CANOE CROSSINGS

SANFORD OSLER

FOREWORD BY SHELAGH ROGERS

CANOE
Understanding the Craft That Helped Shape British Columbia
CROSSINGS

VICTORIA · VANCOUVER · CALGARY

Heritage House Publishing Company Ltd.
heritagehouse.ca

LIBRARY AND ARCHIVES CANADA CATALOGUING IN PUBLICATION

Osler, Sanford, author
Canoe crossings : understanding the craft that helped
shape British Columbia / Sanford Osler.

Includes bibliographical references and index.
Issued in print and electronic formats.
ISBN 978-1-927527-74-0 (pbk.).—ISBN 978-1-927527-75-7 (html).—
ISBN 978-1-927527-76-4 (pdf)

1. Canoes and canoeing—British Columbia—History. 2. Canoes and canoeing—Social aspects—British Columbia—History. 3. British Columbia—History. I. Title.

GV776.15.B7O85 2014   797.12209711   C2013-908468-1   C2013-908469-X

Edited by Lara Kordic
Proofread by Kate Scallion
Cover and book design by Jacqui Thomas
Cover image: *Skookum Kalitan*, by Ed Hill
Frontispiece image by Ed Hill
Chapter opener images: Page 15, based on photograph by Sanford Osler; page 34, based on Royal BC Museum, PN01583BC; page 55, based on photograph on page 131 of John Jennings, *The Canoe: A Living Legend*, Firefly Books, 2002; page 75, based on photograph on page 137 of Roberts and Shackleton, *The Canoe: A History of the Craft from Panama to the Arctic*, Macmillan of Canada, 1983; page 90, based on photograph by Karen Tomlinson; page 117, based on photograph by Sanford Osler of the *Jade Canoe*, by Bill Reid; page 133, based on photograph by Ed Hill.

This book was produced using FSC®-certified, acid-free papers, processed chlorine free, and printed with vegetable-based inks.

Heritage House acknowledges the financial support for its publishing program from the Government of Canada through the Canada Book Fund (CBF), Canada Council for the Arts, and the province of British Columbia through the British Columbia Arts Council and the Book Publishing Tax Credit.

 Canadian Heritage Patrimoine canadien   The Canada Council for the Arts | Le Conseil des Arts du Canada    BRITISH COLUMBIA ARTS COUNCIL

18 17 16 15 14 1 2 3 4 5

Printed in Canada

CONTENTS

To Betty Ann,
my paddling partner on life's journey.

FOREWORD

WHEN I was asked to write the foreword for *Canoe Crossings*, Sanford Osler's lovely debut book, two stories came to mind. One took place on a Sunday morning in late November 2010. I was in Peterborough, Ontario, to visit an elderly friend in the palliative unit of Peterborough General Hospital. She had been suffering from a number of ailments, but it was a broken hip that precipitated her rapid decline. I got to the hospital, only to learn she had died ten minutes before my arrival.

I was bereft. I didn't know what to do or how to react. I paid my respects to her family, got back in the car, and, without thinking, drove to the Canadian Canoe Museum. I parked the car, walked up to the entrance, and read the notice of the museum's hours. It was 10:45 a.m., and the museum didn't open until noon on Sundays. But I pushed the door, and it opened. I explained to the woman at the desk where I had just come from and how I felt I'd been "directed" to come there. She kindly allowed me to wander through the museum. I felt such solace being in the company of the old canoes on display, which had been paddled by people whose spirits still clung to the vessels.

After a while, I heard shouting and giggling and the unmistakable thud of kids running. The place was crawling with children carrying short paddles. They had spent the night in the museum (surely every kid's dream) and were about to decorate those paddles, which they had carved the day before. They were delighted with themselves.

On that day, which had been such a "hard portage," I was reminded of the joy that comes from being around canoes and paddles. I felt my outlook on life return.

—

The second story takes place a few years earlier, in spring 2007, when I was the host of the CBC Radio program *Sounds Like Canada*. One day, the producers and I were kicking around a story idea about the new Seven Wonders of the World. At one point we latched on to the idea of looking for the Seven Wonders of Canada. We launched the search on the radio, and soon listeners from across the country were nominating places, objects, and concepts, from Gros Morne National Park to politeness to poutine.

From thousands of entries, the three-person jury—Chief Roberta Jamieson, rock musician Ra McGuire, and writer Roy MacGregor—chose the final seven wonders: the prairie sky, the Rocky Mountains, Niagara Falls, Old Quebec City, the igloo, Pier 21 —and the canoe.

The canoe was a natural choice. It is central to Canada's history, a beloved symbol, and a vessel that has created happy memories and personal histories for many. Thousands of Canadians voted to name it a Wonder of Canada.

The canoe is a threshold vessel—a skin, a fabric, and some bark between water and sky. Floating is some kind of miracle, some kind of dream. All canoeists are dreamers to a degree. As you will see in the pages ahead, the canoe has always brought diverse groups of people together, both for joy and for common purpose, and it always will.

I love how Sanford Osler is so full of heart as he describes Reconciliation Canada's Canoe Flotilla, held in Vancouver's False Creek in 2013. He says the canoe is a symbol of healing. I believe he is right. Canada has an opportunity to tell a fresh story about the partnership between Aboriginal and non-Aboriginal people. The canoe is a symbol of reconciliation, of people pulling together, "all in the same boat" (as Osler points out), carrying freight, knowing that where we come from is how we got here, navigating obstacles, and moving forward—together. It's a symbol we can rally around to build a new relationship. *Canoe Crossings* lays out all the evidence to make that case. As Chief Robert Joseph of the Gwawaenuk First Nation says, *Namwayut*—"We are all one."

—SHELAGH ROGERS, O.C.,
host of CBC Radio's *The Next Chapter*
and Ambassador at Large for the Canadian Canoe Museum

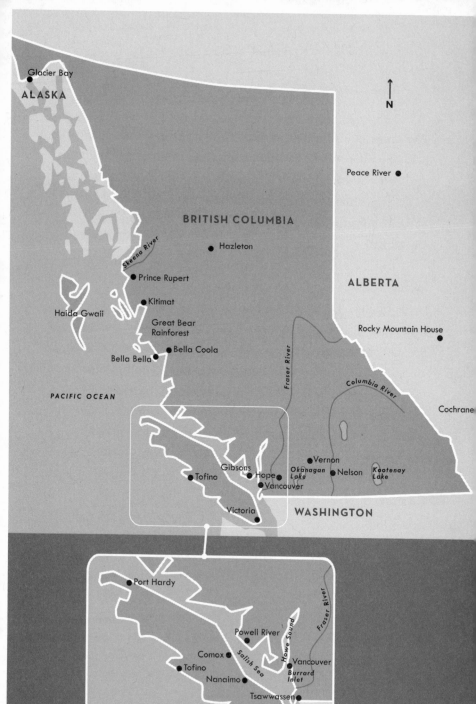

INTRODUCTION

IN 2007, the CBC held a contest to determine the Seven Wonders of Canada—the top natural or man-made places and human creations that have come to embody an essential Canadian-ness. Among the more than twenty thousand nominees were such iconic wonders as the Rocky Mountains, the CN Tower, and the Northwest Passage alongside more unexpected entries such as the Montreal-style bagel, the Narcisse Snake Dens, and the Vegreville Egg. Whereas most of the top choices were firmly situated in or closely tied to a specific province, territory, or region, most did not truly encompass the country as a whole. In a country as geographically vast and diverse as a Canada, it is not surprising that relatively few of our "national" symbols truly represent us all. It's hard to name a person, place, or thing that is equally relevant and meaningful to Quebecers and Yukoners, urbanites and islanders, or Natives and newcomers. It's even more difficult to name something that unites people across the country and is still an active part of our everyday lives, despite its ancient roots.

While nationwide relevance was not one of the criteria of the Seven Wonders contest, one of the judges' final choices did meet all of these conditions. As Peter Mansbridge commented during that year's Canada Day broadcast, "It's hard to imagine Canada being Canada without the canoe. Explorers, missionaries, fur traders and First Nations—they're all linked by this subtle and simple craft. To many, the quintessential Canadian experience begins by picking up a paddle. That's why the canoe is one of the seven wonders."[1]

Not all Canadians agreed, though. Out of the more than one million votes cast in the contest, the canoe's popular-vote ranking was not nearly as high as some of the other nominees'. For example, the canoe's 17,000 votes were dwarfed by the chart-topping 177,000 cast for Thunder Bay's Sleeping Giant (a natural rock peninsula that resembles a giant sleeping on its back). This lack of widespread recognition was reinforced in the results of a 2008 Ipsos Reid survey in which Canadians did not even rank the canoe in the top one hundred things that best defined this country. In that survey, the canoe lost out to Bombardier, Celine Dion, and the Great Lakes, among others.[2] A limited regional breakdown of the results indicated British Columbians also did not place the canoe high on their list of Canadian symbols.[3]

As a lifelong canoe enthusiast, I was surprised and disappointed by the national results. I had always identified the canoe with Canada, and I knew that people in other parts of the world did as well. Australians even refer to birchbark-style canoes as Canadian canoes. But the results in British Columbia probably wouldn't have surprised me if I had heard them twenty years ago when we moved here from Ontario. Back then, my red wooden canoe was sometimes the only one of its type seen on our local trips. At first I thought I had moved away from "canoe country," but over time I came to realize that BC was home to many types of canoes, and was, in fact, the canoe crossroads of Canada—the point at which canoes from all four points of the compass have converged to form what is today a vibrant hub of canoe culture.

I began to suspect, however, that the significance of the canoe in this province was not widely understood or appreciated. Of course, countless people paddle for recreation or fitness, and many are aware of the cultural importance and history of the craft in this province. But relatively few look at the canoe holistically and see the countless ways it has shaped British Columbia and its people. So when I was asked if I wanted to give a talk at my church on the subject of my choosing, I accepted the opportunity to organize my thoughts on canoes and share them with others. I initially thought my presentation would focus on the different types of canoes in BC, but in my research, I began to see much broader themes cutting across the various canoe categories. As I recalled the people I had met and the places I had been, the story began to take on a life of its own.

The talk, complete with my sixteen-foot canoe at centre stage, went well. People said they found it interesting and informative, and they encouraged me to deliver it to other audiences. I added slides to the presentation and proceeded to do just that over the next several years. I was pleased that despite the wide range of audiences, from canoe clubs to Rotary Clubs to Elder College programs, the reaction was positive. Everywhere I went, people would tell me their canoe stories and give me new ideas and leads to pursue. Pretty soon I had much more information than I could fit into a talk, and I began to toy with the idea of writing a book.

The rest, as they say, is history. And the result is the book you are now reading.

In introducing it to you, I should first clarify the terminology. I define "canoe" in a broad way, much as it is used in many parts of the world. The International Canoe Federation (ICF) defines the canoe as "a craft, sharp at both ends, propelled by human power with a paddle either single blade or double bladed where the paddler is facing the direction in which the craft is going."[4] For the purposes of this book, however, I will use Kenneth G. Roberts and Philip Shackleton's definition: "open watercraft of hollow form, generally shaped at each end to improve its hydrodynamic qualities, and designed originally to be propelled by one or more occupants, facing forward and using paddles or push-poles."[5] This means that in addition to the various craft with the word "canoe" in their name, dragon boats and kayaks are included in my canoe family, whereas rowboats and stand-up paddleboards are excluded.

The title of the book, *Canoe Crossings*, was inspired by British Columbia's positioning at the crossroads of canoe culture, alluding to the fact that canoes have converged on British Columbia from all directions. But it also acknowledges that canoes have made long crossings or voyages from British Columbia, trips thousands of kilometres long, and that canoes have crossed various boundaries—between countries and cultures, water and land, urban centres and wilderness, and even the physical and spiritual realms.

This book tells the story of the various types of canoes found in British Columbia, from their first appearance up to the present day, and it examines the various symbolic roles canoes have played in this region. It also looks at the people who have designed and built canoes through the ages, and those who have used them for migration, exploration, hunting, trading, learning, racing, recreation, tourism, and even reconciling differences. I hope you enjoy learning more about the canoes of BC and discovering why this province is truly the canoe crossroads of Canada. I also hope you will learn more about the province and its people and how canoes have fostered creation, development, and healing in BC and beyond.

chapter one —▸

THE BIRCHBARK CANOE

I'VE had an interest in canoes for as long as I can remember. One of the first bedtime stories I recall was Holling C. Holling's *Paddle-to-the-Sea*, a tale of a young First Nations boy who carves a small canoe modelled on his father's birchbark one and launches it in the waters north of Lake Superior. The canoe slowly makes its way through the Great Lakes, surviving various close calls with forest fires, sawmills, and waterfalls, and eventually makes it to the Atlantic Ocean. The story taught me about Canadian geography, history, and natural hazards, but most of all, it taught me about the amazing craft called the canoe—a tiny boat that can travel so far and lead to so many adventures.

My first exposure to a real canoe was at Camp Hurontario on Georgian Bay the summer I was eleven years old. We were taught how to paddle both tandem and solo in wooden canoes. I couldn't get enough of it, particularly paddling alone with the boat well heeled over on its side. It was exhilarating to glide silently over the water. Soon my friends and I were going on overnight trips and using the canoe to explore new territory.

Years later, just before I started at the University of Toronto, four of us went on a two-week canoe trip through Algonquin Provincial Park, starting and finishing at Canoe Lake. This was my longest canoe trip to date, and it exposed us to a variety of conditions and days without seeing other people. It was a taste of wilderness canoeing in a classic Canadian setting. Later, I joined the university's outdoor club and learned whitewater canoeing. Before long, I was running rapids of varying length and difficulty on some of Ontario's finest rivers. I loved the thrill of "shooting the rapids" and the wonderful, fresh smell of the water below them.

When I was in my mid-twenties, I bought a small piece of lakefront property near Algonquin Provincial Park and almost immediately acquired a beautiful red, sixteen-foot, canvas-covered wooden canoe made by the local company Langford Canoes. I loved paddling around the lake, particularly in the calm of the early morning or just before sunset. It was a breathtaking way to experience the sights, sounds, and smells of nature. I was careful not to take that canoe on annual spring whitewater trips, when water flows were at their peak—I think I am still a one-sixth owner of a damaged canoe that my friends and I were forced to buy from the company that rented it to us.

For some of this time, I was dating a girl who worked at nearby Camp Kandalore. During my visits, I met Kirk Wipper, the owner of the camp and canoe collector extraordinaire. Wipper was only too happy to show me around his fledgling canoe "museum" at the camp. He was on his way to gathering what would become the largest collection of canoes in the world, now housed at Peterborough's Canadian Canoe Museum. Shortly after, I went to a presentation on canoeing by Bill Mason, the man whose books and films on canoeing instructed and inspired a whole generation of paddlers. It was only much later that I realized how fortunate I was to meet these two Canadian canoeing icons, both of whom are no longer with us.

Over the next few years, I got married and had two children, and in 1992 we all packed up and moved—along with the canoe—to Vancouver. We lived near the ocean, but the canoe didn't get a lot of use. I didn't think my little canoe belonged on such big water. But when he was ten, my son and I went on a week-long paddle on the Bowron Lake circuit in central BC. This string of connected lakes in beautiful mountainous valleys, replete with moose, wolves, and grizzly bears, opened his eyes to the joys of canoeing and reinvigorated me. The following summer we braved the ocean off Vancouver Island, paddling among the Broken Group Islands with their seals, sea lions, and orca whales. The little red canoe, some forty years old, is now comfortable in the ocean, and I regularly paddle it along our coast during fair summer weather.

One of the places my son and I went with our canoe was the semi-annual gathering of the Northwest Chapter of the Wooden Canoe Heritage Association. This group of canoe lovers focuses on honouring all things related to the original birchbark canoe. The highlight of the weekend was the show-and-tell session, when all the canoes were lined up on the beach and everyone proudly talked about theirs. Our Langford was the only one of its kind, but it fit in well with the other aging craft. The star of the show for me was a real birchbark canoe—a small, light, manoeuvrable craft that I later got to paddle. That weekend reminded me of the rich history of the birchbark canoe and its descendants, and motivated me to delve deeper into its past.

The first Europeans to venture up the Saint Lawrence River in search of a route to Asia more than four hundred years ago were met by a flotilla of canoes. These canoes were made from birchbark and were unlike anything the explorers had seen before. They were lightweight, resilient, and had a high carrying capacity. French explorer Samuel de Champlain described them as "light and elegant as a seagull when it skims the summer waves."[1]

What made these canoes special was the grain of the bark covering them. Unlike all other barks used for canoe building around the world, the grain of a birch tree was transverse (running around the tree trunk) rather than longitudinal (running down the tree trunk). This allowed for sophisticated shaping of the bark and a superior canoe design. In addition, birchbark did not shrink or expand, even when wet; it was smooth and highly resistant to rot.

The birchbark canoe was the foundation of Native existence in much of what we now call Canada. In a land of lakes and rivers, this canoe allowed people to hunt, fish, and trade, as well as explore and wage war. The Europeans quickly recognized the value of these canoes and used them for their own purposes. Champlain wrote that the birchbark canoe was the only craft suitable to navigate the "Upper Country."[2] Indeed, the design of the birchbark canoe was considered so perfect that Europeans used it for the first two hundred years after contact. "Carriages in Canada are canoes made of Birch Bark" was how one European gentleman described it in 1684.[3]

Tappan Adney, who spent his life studying all types of bark canoes and is a respected authority on the subject, recognized the outstanding nature and significance of the birchbark canoe:

> *The adoption by the white man of the Indian's birch bark canoe . . . has no counterpoint anywhere else in the world. So perfectly adapted and of such high order was the material culture of the Natives whom the white discoverers found inhabiting the continent, that they adopted it in*

toto . . . The heavy clumsy European small vessels were utterly useless.[4]

Using birchbark canoes, the Europeans pushed westward. Fur trader Alexander Mackenzie sought a route to the Pacific Ocean to provide easier access to markets. On his first attempt, in 1789, he travelled on the river that now bears his name to the Arctic Ocean. On his second attempt, he successfully reached the Pacific in 1793 via the Peace, Parsnip, Fraser, and Bella Coola Rivers. For most of this trip, he travelled in a twenty-five-foot birchbark canoe that reportedly held ten men and three thousand pounds of freight, yet was light enough that two men could carry it for kilometres without resting.[5] Mackenzie was the first non-Native to travel overland from the Atlantic to the Pacific, and he did the final segment through what is now British Columbia.

Realizing Mackenzie's route was not commercially viable, and knowing of the mouth of the mighty river we now call the Columbia, fur trader Simon Fraser sought a route to the Pacific via that river. He set out in 1808 with twenty-four men in four birchbark canoes. This trip has alternatively been described as "perhaps the most desperate expedition in the history of western exploration"[6] and "probably the most exciting month in the history of the canoe."[7] The river he found was what we now call the Fraser, and it was unnavigable for large stretches. Nevertheless, he and his men did follow it right to present-day Vancouver. It was David Thompson who found and travelled the Columbia River all the way to the Pacific in 1811, arriving two months after the Americans began building a fur-trading post there.

All three of these men had difficulty finding suitable birch trees west of the Rockies and had to switch to other types of canoes to carry on to the ocean. In Thompson's case, he spent over a month at Boat Encampment, where the Canoe and Columbia Rivers meet, designing and building a canoe whose outer layer was made only of cedar planking. As he recorded in March of 1811:

> We had to turn our thoughts to some other material, and Cedar wood being the lightest and most pliable for a Canoe, we split out thin boards of Cedar wood of about six inches in breadth and builded [sic] a Canoe of twenty-five feet in length by fifty inches in breadth, of the same form of a common Canoe, using cedar boards instead of Birch Rind, which proved to be equally light and much stronger than Birch Rind, the greatest difficulty we had was sewing the boards to each round the timbers.[8]

This new type of canoe and its replacements, despite their tendency to leak, carried his group to and from the Pacific. Thompson later built canoes for the British military near Montreal during the War of 1812, and then worked as a mapmaker in Ontario. In 1837, he insisted on using cedar plank canoes for his travels, rejecting the ones made from sheet metal that had been recommended by survey management. He even made his own cedar plank canoes on occasion in Ontario.[9] Canoe historian C. Fred Johnston believed the canoe Thompson made in British Columbia was the inspiration for the cedar plank canoes that began to appear in Ontario in the 1850s.[10]

These early European explorers who made it to the Pacific Ocean were the advance men of the fur trade, the largest and most profitable business in the northern part of the continent for many decades. The Hudson's Bay Company (HBC) was the original company in the industry and initially traded European goods for furs brought by the Aboriginal people to their ships on Hudson Bay each summer. Later, the Scottish-dominated North West Company accessed this fur-rich area by sending canoes from Montreal as far as British Columbia. Both companies primarily sought beaver pelts, which were used to make top hats for fashion-conscious Europeans. The competition and hostility between the two companies increased until they merged under the HBC name in 1821.

The birchbark canoe was key to the fur trade. Aboriginal people used it to transport furs to European traders, who in turn used it to bring the pelts to the ships that sailed to Europe. The essential features of these canoes were a birchbark outer skin sewn to wooden gunwales running along the top of each side and supported by thin cedar planks running lengthwise, and intersecting bent cedar ribs that followed the contour along the bottom and sides of the canoe. Additional strength was provided by several wooden "thwarts" and seats connecting the gunwales.

The fur traders recognized the excellence of this design and retained it, adjusting only the size to meet their needs. For the route between Montreal and Lake Superior, they used the thirty-six-foot *Canot de maître*, also known as the "Montreal canoe," which worked well on the larger rivers and lakes. West of Lake Superior, they switched to the twenty-five-foot *Canot du nord*, or "North canoe," in response to the smaller waterways and the need to carry canoes over more frequent and longer portages.

The fur trade declined as the nineteenth century progressed, but the use of canoes for recreational and sporting purposes increased. As good birchbark became harder and harder to find, people came up with innovative alternatives. A canoe with a painted-sail canvas skin covering a wooden frame was built in Maine in 1882 and proved popular. In addition to being readily available, the canvas was smoother, stronger, and more resilient than birchbark. Canadians Harry and William Chestnut saw one of these canoes and set up the Chestnut Canoe Company in 1907 in New Brunswick to manufacture them. The Peterborough Canoe Company in Ontario was also producing canvas-covered canoes at this time. These two companies were the big names in

Canadian canoe making for decades until the advent of fibreglass and aluminum canoes led to their demise in the 1960s and 1970s. Technical evolutions continued, and ever-more modern materials and production methods were used to make recreational canoes. But the shape and design of the canoe remained fundamentally unchanged from the Aboriginal birchbark version that had been in use for centuries, and the "birchbark-style" canoe is still very much in use today.

—

A critical moment in the transition from wooden frame to fibreglass canoes occurred in 1967. In preparation for Canada's one hundredth birthday, the Chestnut Canoe Company built a dozen twenty-six-foot wood-canvas voyageur canoes for the Centennial Commission, which were tested on a 1966 trip from Montreal to New York. The Commission then asked the company to build fibreglass canoes for a much longer canoe race across Canada. When Chestnut refused, the job went to a Quebec firm that produced fibreglass canoes. The canoes this company built for the Commission followed the voyageur canoe route from Rocky Mountain House to Montreal. Eight provinces, including British Columbia, and two territories had a canoe in the pageant, which took 104 days (still the longest canoe race in history) covering more than five thousand kilometres, including one hundred by portage. These canoes and their descendants would be used to mark the bicentennials of the three European explorers who paddled west, on different routes, in search of the Pacific Ocean.

The first such celebration was the Sir Alexander Mackenzie Canada Sea-to-Sea Bicentennial Expedition that began in Montreal in 1991 and reached Peace River, Alberta, by the end of 1992. In 1993, three fibreglass voyageur canoes set off from the town of Peace River, bound for the Pacific. They reached the Fraser River but their occupants were not able to hike the 350-kilometre trail from the Fraser to Bella Coola, as Mackenzie had done, due to land claim disputes. Interestingly, in 2002, British adventurer Robert Twigger set out from Fort MacKay, south of Lake Athabasca, in a twenty-one-foot birchbark canoe built in Quebec, and reached Bella Coola in 2004, becoming the first person since Mackenzie to succeed in doing so using a traditional craft.

In 2005, representatives from most of the canoes in the Centennial race met for a reunion and hatched the idea of a trip down the British Columbia portion of the Columbia River to commemorate the "discovery" of that river by David Thompson in 1807. Led by Norm Crerar, the Okanagan-based captain of the winning Manitoba team in the 1967 race, the 2007 Columbia River Brigade, named after the group of canoes used by voyageurs, mobilized more than one hundred paddlers in eight voyageur canoes over the course of fourteen days, travelling from the river's headwaters in Columbia Lake to Trail. The following year, the Fort Langley Canoe Club organized a trip with three voyageur canoes that travelled from Fort St. James to Vancouver on the Fraser River to mark the bicentennial of Simon Fraser's journey to the coast in 1808. The same year, a large brigade of ten canoes, including two from BC, travelled the entire voyageur route from Rocky Mountain House to Thunder Bay in sixty-three days, sometimes paddling more than one hundred kilometres in a day, and visiting some forty communities along the way.

The last big, long canoe brigade in BC was the one that took place in 2011 to commemorate David Thompson's Columbia voyage. Marking the two hundredth anniversary of the great land surveyor and mapmaker's descent of the Columbia to its mouth at Astoria, this brigade was an opportunity for the community to engage with their history and renew their relationship with the mighty river. In the nineteenth century, this stretch of river represented the last leg of the fur-trade highway from Montreal to the Pacific, and brigades of laden canoes passed along it regularly.

The brigade involved more than two hundred paddlers in twelve twenty-five-foot voyageur canoes. The sixteen-hundred-kilometre voyage took forty-five days, and the paddlers visited thirty-five communities along the way. The event was designed to be historically evocative, but it was not intended to be an authentic re-creation; modern safety, communication, and other aids were allowed. When they arrived at each community, the paddlers, dressed in period attire, put on a show using advanced manoeuvres. They performed a canoe charge for the spectators on the shore, which was akin to the RCMP Musical Ride, before landing and presenting gifts to the mayor and First Nation chiefs, as well as offering short outings to anyone interested. There was usually a parade, led by the pipers accompanying the brigade that included "David Thompson" himself; a presentation by a scholar on the famed explorer; and traditional dances sparked by the travelling fiddlers.

Although the mood was festive, the event sought to address the river's complex spiritual, recreational, and economic history and its role as a marker of jurisdictional boundaries past and present. It acknowledged both the Aboriginal people who were in power when Thompson first ventured down the river and the settlers who moved in following the historic voyage. In many respects, it is a problematic history, but it is also a history shared by the diverse groups of people who now call the region home.

Week-long voyageur canoe brigades were held on lakes in the Okanagan Valley in 2012 and on the Harrison and Fraser Rivers in 2013. Another series of canoe brigades using the twenty-five-foot North canoes is now in the early planning stages to mark Canada's sesquicentennial in 2017. This time, rather than a race across five provinces, the concept is a series of two-week canoe voyages beginning on July 1 in all regions of the country, followed by a two-week brigade paddling from Toronto to Ottawa.

—

Canoe making in British Columbia has also evolved considerably over the years. Builders of wooden canoes existed throughout the province prior to the 1970s, but they started to go out of business as canoes made of newer materials gained popularity. The biggest and most respected name in west coast wood-canvas canoes was Greenwood. Bill Greenwood visited wooden canoe factories in Maine and Ontario before setting up shop in Vancouver in 1934. His business expanded to include a plant in Richmond, which was destroyed in a fire in 1972. Greenwood canoes came in ten models ranging from thirteen to twenty-five feet. They had a great reputation and were known for their outstanding workmanship and handling excellence. High-quality sitka spruce was used for the ribs, old-growth western red cedar for the planking, and Philippine mahogany for the gunwales. These canoes were wider, more stable, and higher floating than most, making them some of the best for rougher waters.

Just as Bill Greenwood was selling his canoe-making business in 1975, Marlin and Mary Bayes were beginning theirs. School teachers and recreational canoeists, the couple began importing paddles and then bought several canoe moulds from a builder in Mission. Convincing their banker to break his rule of never lending to teachers or for personal hobbies, they started Western Canoeing and Kayaking in Abbotsford. Their Clipper Canoe brand now offers the largest selection of canoes in the world, with more than forty models ranging from fourteen to forty-two feet in length and all made in BC from fibreglass, Kevlar, or basalt. Their canoes are known for their great design and high quality, and the recreational models have several distinguishing characteristics. They are typically deeper than other canoes of similar length, which makes them suitable for paddling through British Columbia's large waves, whether on the ocean or on lakes surrounded by wind-funnelling mountains. The seats in the canoes are typically low for added stability and reflect the Bayes's belief that sitting, with foot and thigh braces, is generally preferable to kneeling, particularly when using the more efficient bent-shaft paddle.

Clipper canoes have also performed well in extreme tests. Two British men paddled a Clipper Tripper, the 17.5-foot model that is the Bayes's biggest seller, from Medicine Hat, Alberta, to the mouth of the Amazon River in Brazil between July 1993 and August 1996. At 22,000 kilometres, it is said to be the longest continual canoe trip ever made.[11] In 1995, another pair made the first successful eight-thousand-kilometre coast-to-coast canoe crossing of Canada in a single paddling season, again using a Clipper Tripper.

Marlin Bayes estimates there have been close to fifty canoe-making companies that have come and gone in BC during the more than thirty-five years he's been in the business. The only other one still in existence in BC of any significant size (albeit much smaller than Western Canoeing) is Hellman Canoes in Nelson.

Bob Hellman moved to Nelson from Manitoba in the early 1990s and, following his passion for canoes, began to build them in his backyard. He eventually bought a shop on Kootenay Lake, which allows him to sell canoes and kayaks in the summer and build canoes in the winter. Hellman canoes are recognized for their quality, come in ten different models from ten to twenty-five feet in length, and are made from tough and lightweight modern materials using designs well suited for BC's varying conditions. Hellman boasts of building the most environmentally friendly canoe in the world, a claim based on the use of an epoxy resin made from plant oils rather than petroleum.

With this better understanding of the evolution of the birchbark canoe, I was curious to learn the fate of Langford Canoes, the builder of my red canoe—the company was suffering when I last dealt with them in 1975. I discovered that it had been sold in the 1980s to people who wanted the land the company owned and who planned to get rid of what was left of the wooden canoe business. However, the new owners found there was a real following of people interested in their canoes and decided to invest in the business. They moved the manufacturing to Quebec, where the voyageur canoes were originally built and canoe-building skills still existed, and they added composite products made of fibreglass, Kevlar, and carbon fibre. They retained beautiful cedar and cedar canvas canoes as their signatures products.

The company has clearly found an appreciative market and become a strong symbol of Canada. In talking with Chris Davidson of Langford, I learned that they produce about five hundred cedar canoes a year, retailing for $4,000 to $6,000, and sell them to customers around the world. Interestingly, the clear cedar-plank canoes are the best sellers. These are essentially the same design as those first built by David Thompson when he couldn't find suitable birchbark in BC. The problem with leaking has been solved by the application of a clear fibreglass cloth on the hull, later coated with watertight epoxy resin—an option not available in Thompson's day. Today, Langford manufactures canoes that are sold under different brand names. For example, prior to the 2010 Olympics in Vancouver, they began producing cedar-canvas canoes for sale at HBC stores, featuring their iconic point blanket colours on the exterior. Billed as a way to "satisfy your inner voyageur," these canoes now also sell at Lord and Taylor stores in the US.

Langford calls itself "Canada's oldest canoe company," having been in existence since 1940, and the only one still making cedar canoes in any quantity. In fact, Davidson wasn't aware of any canoe maker in the world that came close to making as many wooden canoes as Langford. "People from all over the world [are] calling you and they associate canoeing and everything in Canada with the company . . . They want a red canoe from Canada," Langford president Steve MacAllister said in a 2011 interview with the *Globe and Mail*.[12] And the cedar planking in their highest-quality, world-famous canoes comes from British Columbia.

While wooden canoes are still being made and restored on a very small scale in BC, the commercial production of true birch-bark canoes has essentially ceased in Canada. The vast majority of birchbark-style canoes manufactured today are of modern, lightweight, and lower-maintenance materials, and are the ones owned by many Canadian households. You can imagine my surprise, then, when I saw twelve "birchbark" canoes, complete with stereotypical voyageurs, dance across the floor during the Closing Ceremony of the 2010 Olympic Games. They were a part of a final send-off using iconic Canadian symbols including Mounties, hockey players, beavers, and moose.

Several days later I got a note from James Raffan, executive director of the Canadian Canoe Museum. The museum, based in Peterborough, Ontario, is now the repository of the canoe collection that Kirk Wipper started, and it has the largest collection of paddling craft in the world. James had seen the Closing Ceremony on TV and wanted to know how the museum could get one of those canoes. I told him the Olympic memorabilia was being auctioned off to the public and wished him luck.

About a week later I got a call from James saying the museum had been the successful bidder on one of the canoes. He said it had to be picked up within three days and asked if I could do that and store the canoe until he had arranged how to transport the canoe more than four thousand kilometres from Vancouver to the museum. I agreed and had great fun picking up the canoe, which turned out to be fibreglass with a realistic birchbark design painted on the exterior. It also had two big square holes in the bottom, which allowed each "voyageur" to carry and dance it across the floor. I got some very funny looks as I drove home with a canoe that had two large holes in it on top of my car.

Inspecting the canoe more closely, I saw that it was made by North Woods Canoe Company of Cochrane, Alberta, so I called to find out more about this strange craft. President Larry Meriam has a strong personal interest in the canoes of the fur-trade era, and his company builds many specialty canoes of historical significance. He chuckled as he recalled his top-secret work on the twelve dancing canoes, and the challenges of building something that met the artistic need to look like an authentic voyageur canoe, was light enough to "dance," and was strong enough to remain intact with two large holes. He was happy with the results and pleased to hear that one of the canoes was destined for the Canadian Canoe Museum.

After several weeks of patiently waiting for the mover to show up and free up space in our now overcrowded garage, I contacted James. He said he had found a Peterborough-based mover who was willing to take the canoe back from Vancouver, free of charge, next time he was there and had space in a truck. No such trips were on the roster, but James was hopeful one would happen soon. My wife, who had gone to school with James, was skeptical and insisted I free up the space in the garage. That is why an eighteen-foot simulated birchbark canoe with two big holes in it sat on our front lawn for much of the summer, much to the amusement of our friends and neighbours.

As the grass died, my wife grew increasingly unhappy with the huge lawn ornament, and as the story of the strange canoe spread, a canoeing buddy told me of a friend who owned a trucking company that might be able to help. Mary Waring was most willing to assist, and before long the canoe got a free trip to Ontario inside a huge transport truck. I visited the canoe the next time I was at the museum and was told it had been a real hit there—dancing at their annual Beaver Club Gala, marching in the local Canada Day parade, and generally having a lot of fun. It's interesting to contemplate the variety of roles this one canoe has played in the course of a year.

———

In October of 2011, I went to an event in Vancouver involving voyageur canoes that was also a lot of fun. Billed as the largest voyageur canoe race in the world, Day of the Longboat is an annual event organized by the University of British Columbia (UBC) Recreation Department. The year I attended was its twenty-fifth anniversary, and a record 350 teams paddled fibreglass voyageur canoes in heats of ten canoes along an ocean course.

I spent several hours taking in the atmosphere and talking to participants. Team spirit was high; members wore matching costumes, painted their faces, and adorned themselves to reflect names such as Space Cowboys, Club Moose, and Team Haida. There seemed to be a real cross-section of the community with different cultures, faculties, and groups participating. Some teams represented already existing units, while others were made up of individuals that came on their own. Many of the participants had never canoed before, as evidenced by several collisions and the odd canoe dumping throughout the course of the event. But everyone seemed to have fun, and a hot tub warmed up those who had spent time in the cold Pacific.

Intrigued, I tracked down Dr. Nestor Korchinsky, the now-retired long-time director of intramural sports at UBC, who was behind the whole thing, to learn more. He happily agreed to have lunch with me and fill me in on the background of the event.

When he was hired by UBC in 1967, Korchinsky was shocked to find that despite the university's fine reputation across the country, the students did not appear to have pride in their own school. Korchinsky concluded that "UBC did not have a soul" and resolved to do what he could to help the university find it. He sought to develop a program to engage as many people as possible and create a sense of identity at the university. He wanted events that were unique, took advantage of the local geography, and reflected First Nations culture. In a meeting with Kirk Wipper in Toronto in the 1980s on another matter, he learned about Wipper's involvement in acquiring an important old canoe from BC, and "the wheels started to turn." After exploring several ways of creating a canoe-based activity, the Day of the Longboat was born and has grown ever since. Based on the twenty-fifth incarnation of this unique event, with its thousands of spirited and engaged people from on and off campus, I would assert he has indeed helped the university improve its sense of community and discover its soul.

The idea of the canoe facilitating a sense of community can be extended back to the role the birchbark canoe played in the formation of British Columbia. The canoe enabled Alexander Mackenzie to reach the Pacific in the northern part of today's province and Simon Fraser to reach it in the southern part. They were both looking for a cheaper way to get furs to market and to ensure they would not have to cross any international borders with the attendant tariffs on their goods. Subsequent fur traders sought to keep as much of the west coast in British hands as possible. The Russians were pushing southward from Alaska and claimed the territory down to the fifty-first latitude, near the top of Vancouver Island. Using the slogan "fifty-four forty or fight," the Americans were pushing northward with the goal of reaching the fifty-fourth parallel, north of Prince Rupert. Largely because of the presence of HBC forts and the company's steamship *Beaver* operating along the coast, the current boundaries were defined. The Russians were held to the Alaska Panhandle and Canada's southern boundary was extended west from the Rockies on the forty-ninth latitude, dipping south to include all of Vancouver Island and HBC's Fort Victoria. Without the canoe-enabled fur trade, British Columbia would almost certainly have had a smaller area and coastline.

How was it that such a small number of Europeans in the northern half of the continent were able to gain control of such a vast area extending all the way to the Pacific? Much of the answer lies in the unusual partnership between the Europeans and Aboriginal people, which was largely based on the canoe.

Samuel de Champlain, who founded New France and Quebec City in 1608, had an attitude toward indigenous people that was rare for Europeans in those days. Concerned with the treatment of the Native population he observed in the Spanish colonies, he concluded the key to a successful French colony along the Saint Lawrence was to learn how to live and travel in this wilderness from the Aboriginal population. His ultimate goal was to establish a new world where people of different cultures could live together in harmony. This was at a time when other Europeans were debating whether the Natives of North America were animals or humans, and regarded cohabiting with them as treasonous and sinful.

Champlain's philosophy led naturally to the development of the fur trade. The Native people taught the Europeans the way of the birchbark canoe for travelling and communicating in the wilderness. They brought the French furs that could be transported back to Europe in return for various goods of value to them. This mutually beneficial business relationship was cemented by intermarriage between French settlers and Natives, another radical idea championed by Champlain, and the beginning of the Métis population. This approach by the French was unique in North America, and the accompanying military alliances with the Native people allowed France to maintain military superiority until its defeat on the Plains of Abraham in 1759. Even after the British victory, the military alliances with the Native population continued and enabled the defeat of the American invasion in the War of 1812, which in turn led to the establishment of the forty-ninth parallel as the international border west of Lake of the Woods.

The fur trade, meanwhile, evolved to include a mix of Scottish, French, Métis, and Native cultures, and continued to push westward by canoe. Compared to the westward expansion by the Americans, relations between European and indigenous populations north of the forty-ninth parallel were relatively good and non-violent. Alexander Mackenzie learned of the route to the Pacific from the Native people. Simon Fraser could never have done his trip to the coast without co-operation from First Nations. David Thompson had his Métis wife, Charlotte Small, with him for much of his exploration work. What began as a new approach in dealing with Native people became the basis for the establishment of an empire that stretched to three oceans. The birchbark canoe was the vehicle and way of life that tied it together for centuries.

John Ralston Saul in his 2009 book, *A Fair Country: Telling Truths about Canada*, argues that early European settlers' novel decision to partner with the Aboriginal people and adopt the canoe has had a profound impact on Canada's identity and values. He links Canadians' interest in egalitarianism, consensus seeking, peacemaking, medicare, and multiculturalism, among other concepts, to a heavy Aboriginal influence. So the simple canoe may have not only helped define Canada as a country, but also may have shaped our very nature as a people.

chapter two —

THE DUGOUT CANOE

UNTIL we moved to Vancouver in 1992, the birchbark canoe and its closely related successors were what came to mind when I thought of an open canoe. This was the dominant style of canoe throughout much of Canada, and it had played a key role in the history I had learned in school. It seemed like such a natural craft for the rivers and lakes that were so prevalent in the country.

My opinion changed one September afternoon when I attended a local festival to honour the return of the Pacific salmon. Pulled up on the beach was a magnificent black dugout canoe about thirty feet long. I talked to some of the canoe's paddlers and learned it was recently designed and built by members of the local Squamish Nation. Our conversation was cut short as a procession of dignitaries, followed by the crowd, converged on the canoe as it was launched and set out to sea to complete the official salmon-blessing ceremony.

This canoe, which was very much at home in the world's largest ocean, was a revelation to me. When I realized that "canoe" and "ocean" were anagrams, the idea didn't seem quite so strange anymore. And learning that both Alexander Mackenzie and Simon Fraser had cached their birchbark canoes and finished their pioneering journeys to the coast in local dugout canoes provided a historical link between the two types of craft for me. I was determined to learn more about these beautiful canoes.

———

Prior to contact with Europeans, Northwest Coast culture was one of the most complex Native cultures on the continent, if not the world. Much of this sophistication was due to the resources in the region, particularly the western red cedar and the Pacific salmon. The traditional west coast dugout canoe, carved from a single cedar tree, was probably the most important aspect of Northwest Coast culture.

These canoes were used for a variety of purposes, including harvesting seals, whales, and fish; transporting people and goods; and waging war. They operated on rivers, inland seas, and the open ocean. They ranged from short, single-person craft to ones more than sixty feet long that could carry dozens of people. They were essential and integral to the economic, cultural, and spiritual life of these communities.

Every coastal First Nations group designed and built dugout canoes based on available resources and suited to their purposes and environment. The biggest canoe makers were likely the Haida Nation. They had the greatest need, being island people, and the best trees. One of their chief exports was, in fact, canoes. They have been called the "Phoenicians of the Northern Pacific"[1] and the "Vikings of the coast."[2]

Particularly awe-inspiring are the Haida ocean-going war canoes. Generally ranging from thirty-five to sixty-five feet in length, these majestic canoes were used to travel the more than eighty treacherous kilometres separating Haida Gwaii from the mainland, as well as along the coast. Beautiful craft, particularly when finished with artwork, they also had some advanced design features. They were incredibly buoyant—so much so that they needed ballast for stability if not fully loaded. The long and high pieces at the bow and stern allowed for a smoother ride in big waves. The vertical cutwater under the prow threw off high waves when going upwind and kept the canoe going straight, rather than twisting, when going downwind with a following sea. Complementing these features were well-developed steering and paddling methods that allowed paddlers to survive in rough seas.

Kenneth Roberts and Philip Shackleton thought highly of these canoes and canoeists. In their book, *Canoe: A History of the Craft from Panama to the Arctic*, they write, "The master mariners of the coast—the Haidas, the Kwakiutls and the Nootkas—met the challenge of [the North Pacific] by producing canoes unrivalled for their seaworthy qualities and by proving themselves seamen of extraordinary boldness and skill."[3] Similarly, Hilary Stewart, in tracing the uses of western red cedar, wrote, "Nowhere else in the world was a dugout [canoe] developed to such a degree of sophistication; no other people had a dugout that could match the speed, capacity and seaworthiness—or the elegant grace—of the sleek canoes of the Northwest Coast Indian."[4]

The first Europeans to reach the Northwest Coast did so by sea in the latter part of the eighteenth century and were impressed with both the quality and quantity of dugout canoes that greeted them. An officer of the Spanish ship *Sutil* in 1792 reported that the First Nations–built canoes were "so exactly proportioned that they are extremely light and strong and very well shaped. Men and women alike manage these canoes well in the sea."[5] Captain Thomas Barnett recorded that six hundred Haida canoes surrounded his trading ship in Haida Gwaii in 1791.[6] Indeed, there were thought to be enough canoes on the coast at that time to hold the entire estimated population of up to 100,000 people, along with many of their worldly goods.[7]

At first, the canoes flourished after Europeans arrived. The large demand for sea otters, initially called sea beavers by the Europeans, was met by the First Nations operating from their dugout canoes. When overharvesting led to the sea otters' near extinction, the demand shifted to fur seals, also hunted from canoes. The early missionaries who lived with the coastal people were clearly awed by the dugout canoes they saw. Archbishop William Collison, the first missionary in Haida Gwaii, described the first time he saw a fleet of Haida canoes approaching the shore in 1874:

> The fleet consisted of some forty large canoes, each with two snow-white sails spread, one on either side of each canoe, which caused them to appear like immense birds or butterflies, with white wings outspread, flying shorewards. Before a fresh westerly breeze they glided swiftly onward over the rolling waves, which appeared to chase each other in sport as they reflected the gleams of the summer's sun. These were the Masset Haida, who were famed for their fine war canoes. They have always been the canoe builders of the northern coast.[8]

Later, in 1877, Archbishop Collison observed an impressive array of recently constructed canoes assembled along the shore:

> Some of them were large, some of medium size, and some small, ranging from fifty feet in length and six and a half feet beam, down to half this size and less. The largest were

*for ocean travelling and freight, and resembled the old war
canoes while those of medium size were used for hunting
the fur seal and sea otter. All were perfect in outline and
beautiful in construction.*[9]

The tide began to turn in the nineteenth century. Smallpox
and other European-introduced diseases decimated the Native
population, while the missionaries and government agents sought
to destroy Native culture and traditions. The potlatch, a gift-giving
festival that depended heavily upon dugout canoes, was banned
in 1884. Residential schools, designed to assimilate Native children into mainstream culture, were introduced in the 1870s. These
changes, along with the decline and eventual closing of fur seal-
ing, led to a sharp reduction in the need for new dugouts. Later, in
the twentieth century, existing canoes were redesigned to accommodate the new gas-powered outboard motors, and new boats
were made from planks—a cheaper and faster method. Even the
maritime environment changed as the collapse of the sea otter
population led to the decline of the long lines of kelp beds that
had provided more sheltered channels for coastal travel.

Interestingly, the new settlers did find some other uses for the
dugout canoes. Some helped transport gold seekers to the Interior.
One fifty-year-old dugout served as the hull for the *Tilikum*, the
sailboat that made the world-record 64,000-kilometre voyage
from Victoria, BC, westward to Europe, in less than forty months
(between 1901 and 1904). John Voss, the *Tilikum*'s designer and
captain, described the Vancouver Island dugout canoe he used as
"one of nature's wonders." The resulting sailboat was relatively narrow and light, sailed very well, and made better time than many
deep and heavy ocean cruisers.

The shape of the ocean-going dugout canoes may also have
influenced the design of later ships. The first European vessels to visit

the Northwest Coast were blunt and round at the front. Subsequent ships such as the fast clipper sailing ship and the Atlantic greyhound steamer had hull shapes much closer to that of the coastal canoe.

The making of ocean-going dugout canoes essentially stopped for much of the twentieth century. The last great Haida war canoe was a fifty-six-foot vessel, built in 1908, which now rests in the Canadian Museum of History (formerly called the Canadian Museum of Civilization) in Gatineau, Quebec.

—

Kirk Wipper understood the historical significance of Northwest Coast canoes and wanted one for his fledging canoe museum. He learned that Victor Adams, a Haida carver living at the once-great canoe-making centre of Masset, on Haida Gwaii, would be willing to build one. It took Adams three years to rediscover and apply traditional canoe-making techniques. He wrote to Wipper at one point, "We haven't done this for so long that it's hard to know whether we're doing it right."[10] Launched amid much local interest in 1971, the twenty-six-foot *Eagle* eventually made its way to Camp Kandalore with James Raffan at the helm. No more canoes were built at Masset that century.

The man who did succeed in resurrecting the art of building large ocean-going canoes on the Northwest Coast was Bill Reid. Born in 1920 to Haida mother and a father of Scottish-German descent, Reid learned of his Native heritage only in his twenties; his mother's residential schooling had led her to be ashamed of and suppress her background. A talented artist and communicator, Reid began designing and making First Nations–inspired jewellery and then large cedar totem poles. It was the canoe that really captured his attention. He believed that west coast Native art starts with that craft: "The Haida canoe is as beautifully designed and decorated an open boat as the world has ever seen."[11]

Building a big ocean-going canoe for the first time in almost a century was no easy task. Researching the project involved studying the dozens of incomplete canoes in the Haida Gwaii forest, casualties of the smallpox-induced population collapse, as well as the few remaining finished ones. Reid built two prototypes; the larger, twenty-four-foot canoe is now on display at the Museum of Anthropology at the University of British Columbia. The final fifty-foot canoe, called *Lootaas* or "wave eater" in the Haida language, was launched in Skidegate on Haida Gwaii in time for a triumphant entrance at the opening of Vancouver's Expo '86. Later, four fibreglass replicas—what Bill Reid referred to as his "Tupperware fleet"—were built, one of which, *Black Eagle*, is on the grounds of Vancouver's VanDusen Botanical Garden.

As spectacular as its role was in Vancouver, *Lootaas*'s most important trip was its voyage to Haida Gwaii in 1987. During this nineteen-day trip, *Lootaas* stopped at many communities that hadn't seen such a canoe in most people's memories. The coastal First Nations relearned receiving protocols, held celebratory feasts, and rekindled pride in their canoe heritage. Haida paddler Andy Wilson reminisced about the historic 1987 journey:

> *Thanks to Bill [Reid], we . . . not just the Haida people, but the people up and down the coast, were able to reconnect because they had to learn their songs and their dances to welcome the Haida into their big houses. So it wasn't just one group of people doing something, reconnecting with their past, but it was a whole coast, where they had to relearn their protocol, their song and dances. And there was a whole dynamic of reaching into the past for everybody. So it was a pretty spectacular time for us . . .*
>
> *It's a connection to our ancestors. And Bill was that vital, important connection for us in the present to our ancestors in the past.*[12]

Lootaas's next big trip was to France in 1989, where it was paddled nine hundred kilometres up the Seine River and made a dramatic entrance to Paris. Noted French anthropologist Claude Lévi-Strauss had classified the art of the Northwest Coast among the five great artistic traditions of human history.[13] Reid wanted to show the coastal canoe as part of a living Haida culture in one of the great art centres of the world. After a welcome by Jacques Chirac, then the mayor of Paris, *Lootaas* was carefully manoeuvred into the Musée de l'Homme to join a special exhibition in honour of Lévi-Strauss.

Lootaas completed the circle with its creator when it transported Bill Reid's remains to his ancestral birthplace in Haida Gwaii after his death in 1998. This seemed a fitting end for someone who had said that he had got "more satisfaction out of the building of [*Lootaas*] than of anything I've ever done."[14] Indeed, *Lootaas* was a metaphor for Bill Reid's recognition and reclamation of what it meant to be Haida.

Bill Reid may have revived the ability to make large ocean-going canoes and rekindled an interest in the vessels along the coast, but it was a young man from Bella Bella, a mid-coast island community, who caused that interest to take root. Frank Brown was a Native youth headed for juvenile detention after several run-ins with the law when his aunt asked the judge to sentence him to the traditional Native punishment of banishment. Alone on an island, Brown rediscovered himself and his roots and became dedicated to promoting his heritage. He spearheaded the building and paddling of a dugout canoe from Bella Bella to Vancouver for Expo '86 and was one of the few Canadians to participate in the 1989 Paddle to Seattle, a local event to celebrate Washington State's one hundredth anniversary. At the end of the celebration, he invited all the nations to paddle to Bella Bella in 1993. He spent the next four years planning the festival and visiting communities up and down the coast to raise awareness of and encourage participation in the event. In the end, twenty-three canoes travelled to Bella Bella, some paddling more than eight hundred kilometres, in what was a transformative event for many. Tom Heidlebaugh spent two and a half months on the journey from the Olympic Peninsula to Bella Bella and back, and he wrote:

> Elders wept as we brought the canoes in to ancient and accustomed beaches along the way. They saw the raised sails and remembered the family journeys of their youth, when young girls sat in the middle of the canoe weaving baskets as the adults pulled them to feasts or fishing sites. "You are a gift to us," they said. "We never thought we'd see the great canoes again."[15]

The Bella Bella experience was so successful that the canoe journey and gathering, now known as the Tribal Journeys (or Canoe Journey), became a regular event. Initially held every four years, it is now an annual event. Communities throughout BC, Washington, and even Oregon have taken their turn hosting it. Frank Brown is again organizing the Qatuwas canoe festival to be held in Bella Bella in 2014—the first time a community has hosted the event twice. The 2014 Tribal Journeys brochure assesses the impact of the Journeys as follows: "For more than 20 years the Tribal Journeys have transformed the lives of thousands of aboriginal youth. It has helped them to reconnect to their culture and has strengthened their confidence as contemporary First Nations people."[16] Word of Tribal Journeys has spread internationally, and other indigenous groups such as the Maori from New Zealand, native Hawaiians, and the Ainu from Japan now participate.

I had the good fortune to see the canoes arrive in Cowichan Bay on southeastern Vancouver Island in July 2008. More than one hundred canoes, a record number for Tribal Journeys, arrived from sixty-five points of origin, ranging from Alaska to Oregon. They were organized into groups—those from the north, south, east, and west—and the canoes in each group proudly paddled past the hundreds of welcoming spectators on the spit before seeking permission to land from the local chief, in a request such as this one:

> *We are the Elwha S'Klallam Nation. In the name of the Creator of all good things, we come in peace. We have travelled a great distance to be with you, to honour your people, to respect your waters, and to know this land. We bring greetings from our nations to the south. Like our ancestors, we move carefully on this voyage. We have learned some things and we have come to share with your people so we can learn more. Our hearts are filled with love for you. May we have permission to come ashore?*[17]

The ceremony was quite a sight. The size, shape, and type of canoes varied considerably, as did their colour and artwork. The paddlers were of all ages and wore a range of outfits, including ceremonial dress. The paddles, too, varied in shape, material, and adornments. Once all the canoes had been officially welcomed, everyone was invited to the great feast that the hosts had arranged, and singing and dancing by the various nations carried on for days.

It's hard to overstate the importance of these Tribal Journeys. For the individuals involved, most of whom are Aboriginal youth, the experience begins during the months of training before the journey to help them prepare physically, mentally, emotionally, and spiritually. The actual journey, conducted in an environment free of drugs, alcohol, or tobacco, provides them with an opportunity to discover themselves and their potential role and direction in life.

At Cowichan Bay, I heard young people telling others that the experience had changed their lives and that it had been the "best thing in the world." Lela May Morganroth wrote, "Travelling in our canoe we're doing it as our ancestors did it a long time ago, and it gives us more spirit and power through our hearts and through our minds, and it changes a lot of people."[18] Another woman reported emotionally on the impact within her family: "Drinking means nothing to my son now. All he wants to do is get in that canoe. He's out on the water, paddling. He wants to carve. He wants to know the cedar."[19]

Participants learn to work together and support each other during the challenges they face during the journey. They learn to function as a team, using drumming, singing, and storytelling to maintain their rhythm and work as one. This is in line with Native tradition, according to Chief Justin George: "The elders say that one must always respect the spirit of the canoe, and that all who sit in the canoe set aside differences and focus on pulling together for the greater good of the journey, with one heart, one mind and one spirit."

At the community level, the experience helps the youth better understand and respect their history and their ancestors as they retrace ancient paths. And every evening, as they are welcomed with elaborate ceremonies that last well into the night at the various points along the journey, they gain a better knowledge of, and pride in, their culture and heritage. Some have called it the rebirth of their culture. Peggy Ahvakana of Washington State sees the canoe as a physical embodiment of her ancient culture and a means of relearning the traditional ways of life that had been forgotten through decades of colonialism. "The sacredness of the cedar is a living thing," she wrote. "It stands obedient, then is taken and transformed into another form of teacher." This concept of a canoe as a teacher is beautifully illustrated in the lessons learned by those who participate in Tribal Journeys: "What you do get are some lessons on how to live your life, be centred, how you fit into your tribe, your community, as well as how others around you fit into your community. It's a great gift to be able to learn from the cedar tree that you do matter, that you do count."[20] Bill Wasden of Alert Bay expressed similar sentiments: "The canoe is so very important to our culture. It seems to be a healing tool, especially for the youth . . . I think in our modern world the canoe is going to lead the way. It's bringing our youth back to our culture."[21]

Beyond the community, the canoe gatherings have bridged relationships between the various coastal nations in a way that has been difficult to do since potlatches were outlawed in 1884. Indeed, the journeys offer an opportunity to exchange dialogue, find common ground, and forge new groupings. One chief expressed the effect of this newfound unity: "Where we once were many nations, fighting among each other, struggling with Canadian and American laws and dealing with the loss of land and fishing and timber rights, now those days are gone. Something has happened with this journey [to Bella Bella]. Where once there were many nations of us, there is now one Canoe Nation."[22]

Finally, the journeys helped the nations develop greater respect for the environment and reconnect with nature—from an appreciation of the cedar tree from which their canoes were made to the tides, weather, and marine life that affected their travel. Some of the canoes on the Tribal Journeys have recently been used in scientific research on ocean water quality. They make ideal testing vessels because of their slow speed, smooth movement through the water, and lack of toxic emissions.[23]

The west coast became home to another important canoe journey in the 1990s. Roy Henry Vickers, a First Nations artist born on the Nass River north of Prince Rupert, and Ed Hill, another artist and RCMP staff sergeant, teamed up to define a vision of raising funds to build an addiction recovery centre in BC. Both men were in recovery from substance abuse; Vickers had been treated at a top US addiction recovery centre and Hill was a rehabilitated alcoholic.

Roy Vickers knew the power of the canoe to unite a community and rekindle its spirit, and he recognized the potential of a canoe journey to raise awareness and funds for such a centre. He also knew of the difficulty for some Northwest Coast communities to build, operate, and maintain their own dugout canoes. On a trip to Hawaii, he saw how well modern outrigger canoes had caught on with young people. He approached Western Canoeing and Kayaking in Abbotsford about the possibility of designing and building a modern ocean-going dugout-style canoe. James van Nostrand, a top canoe designer working for the company who had been at the canoe festival in Bella Bella in 1993, was up to the challenge. He created the Northern Dancer, a thirty-one-foot Haida-style canoe made of fibreglass. A fraction of the weight of the cedar-carved dugouts and less vulnerable to damage, they were ideal for a journey in support of a BC recovery centre.

RCMP management also saw the value of such a journey in building bridges and improving relations with First Nations communities. The challenge they faced in this endeavour was reflected in the Native word for police officer, consistently translated among the many languages on the West Coast as "the man who takes you away"—harking back to an era when even some forms of singing and dancing were punishable by imprisonment.[24] The canoe served as a metaphor for the RCMP's new emphasis on being a community resource, and they endorsed what became known as the VisionQuest project.

Three new Northern Dancer canoes set out on a sixteen-hundred–kilometre journey from Hazelton to Victoria in the summer of 1997. The trio headed down the Skeena River before going south along the coast. Days typically started around four or five o'clock a.m. and involved many hours of paddling before the paddlers changed into red serge dress uniforms for a huge, elaborate, and emotional welcoming ceremony and feast at a new community. Tears were shed by both the paddlers and hosts before they headed to bed after midnight. Despite the demanding schedule, difficult conditions, and accumulating sleep deprivation, the flotilla arrived in Victoria a month later, after joining with the Tribal Journey in time for the start of the North American Indigenous Games.

For Roy Vickers, the trip stimulated dialogue about substance abuse and addiction, which affected many of the people in the communities the paddlers visited, as well as raised hope and funds for a recovery centre. For the RCMP, the canoe journey helped raise awareness about addiction, which is at the root of a lot of criminal activity, and it helped the police force overcome its past reputation and improve relations with Native communities. And for many of the participants, the trip was a healing spiritual journey. In support of VisionQuest, musician David Foster wrote the song "River of Love," whose lyrics allude to the unity of all nations.

Ursula Vaira, one of the paddlers on VisionQuest, penned the following poem about the experience:

The grandfathers' journey

has not been done by canoe in a hundred years.
That is because the knowledge and the will

to build these canoes were long ago smashed
by Mounties made to do the government's dirty work.

They burned the longhouses and the regalia
and the art of ritual, arrested those who potlatched,

dragged children out of their homes to the residential schools,
leaving fathers and mothers with no reason to carry on.

At each community the RCMP will sit still,
have their sins named by grandmothers,

by grandfathers, by parents of teen suicides,
by the children peeking out from the chiefs' robes.

Then Inspector John Grant, hardened veteran,
poet and brave man, will stand and apologize for

"those acts which, although sanctioned
by law at the time, were morally wrong."

After that, the pullers are promised,
there will be feasting.[25]

The event deeply affected both the RCMP officers and the members of the communities they visited, particularly the elders in isolated communities, many of whom hadn't seen a traditional dugout canoe since childhood. For the fifty RCMP officers who participated in the voyage, it was a gesture of remorse, goodwill, and reconciliation. Inspector John Grant referred to it as "probably the most important trip the RCMP ever made since the march west in 1873."[26]

For Ed Hill, the VisionQuest journey had been a profoundly moving experience. He was awed by the way it helped to improve relationships between the police and Aboriginal communities. He was later invited to paddle the RCMP canoe on the Fraser River at Hope. Hill committed to bringing a fleet of canoes in future, and in 2001 he led the first Pulling Together Journey of big canoes from Hope to Gibsons. The trip was a success, leading to the creation of the Pulling Together Canoe Society and annual canoe journeys. Participation broadened to include other police and federal authorities and, on the Aboriginal side, focused more

The author and his son get a close look at a moose during a trip through the Bowron Lakes. The world-class canoe circuit in central BC also supports black and grizzly bears, caribou, and wolves. SANFORD OSLER

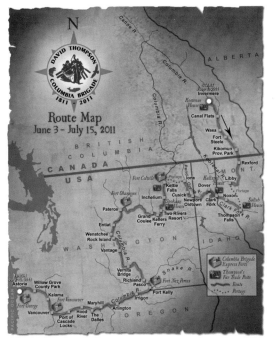

A map of the route followed by the David Thompson Columbia Brigade, following closely the original journey by the explorer exactly two hundred years earlier.

MAP BY MICHAEL DIXON OF RASTRO GRAPHICS, COURTESY OF ROSS MACDONALD

Canoes from the Thompson Columbia Brigade in 2011 near Wasa, BC, as they re-create Thompson's journey by canoe from the headwaters of the Columbia River to its mouth on the Pacific Ocean. ROSS MACDONALD

Members of the Thompson Columbia Brigade put on a show in their canoes as they arrive at Invermere. ROSS MACDONALD

The Descent of the Fraser, 1808, from a colour drawing by C.W. Jefferys, 1915.

One of the "dancing" canoes used in the closing ceremony of the 2010 Winter Olympics in Vancouver. The author received many surprised looks when transporting this craft around Vancouver. SANFORD OSLER

The start of one heat of the University of British Columbia's annual Day of the Longboat race. The race involves more than three thousand paddlers and is described as the largest voyageur canoe race in the world. CARTER BRUNDAGE, COURTESY OF UBC RECREATION

The leading canoes approach the finish line of the Day of the Longboat race in 2011. CARTER BRUNDAGE, COURTESY OF UBC RECREATION

Dugout canoes and Captain James Cook's ships in Nootka Sound, Vancouver Island, in March 1778. LIBRARY AND ARCHIVES CANADA, C-011201

This fifty-foot Haida dugout canoe was built prior to 1904. The painting on the side depicts a small killer whale on the bow and a larger one on the main body. ROYAL BC MUSEUM, PN01583BC

Tilikum, built atop an old dugout canoe found on Vancouver Island, at anchor in the tropics in 1901 en route from Victoria, BC, to London, England.
CITY OF VANCOUVER ARCHIVES BO P369

Bill Reid's fifty-foot ocean-going dugout canoe, *Lootaas*, built for Expo '86, carrying the Olympic torch off Haida Gwaii in November 2009.
HEATHER RAMSAY, COURTESY OF THE *HAIDA GWAII OBSERVER*

Inspired by *Lootaas*, newly carved ocean-going dugout canoes head south towards Victoria as part of the 1997 Tribal Journeys. HUGH WESTHEUSER

The first three Northern Dancers, fibreglass canoes modelled on North Coast ocean-going canoes and made by Western Canoeing and Kayaking. ED HILL

Masked Kwak'waka'wakw dancers
perform in the bows of their dug-
out canoes as they enter Victoria's
Inner Harbour at the close of
Tribal Journeys.
DAVID NEEL, DAVID NEEL STUDIO

Roy Henry Vickers and John Grant, leaders of the 1,600-kilometre Vision-Quest journey from Hazelton to Victoria in 1997. ED HILL

RCMP and First Nations paddlers on the VisionQuest journey, which sought to raise funds for a recovery centre in BC and improve relations between the RCMP and First Nations people. ED HILL

Canoes from VisionQuest and Tribal Journeys converge on Victoria for the 1997 North American Indigenous Games, where they are greeted by some twenty thousand people. UNKNOWN PHOTOGRAPHER, COURTESY OF ED HILL

The Pulling Together canoe fleet approaches Powell River in 2012 with a BC Ferry, coast guard support boat, and the mountains of Vancouver Island in the background. ED HILL

The Pulling Together canoe fleet on Okanagan Lake in 2009.

The Sunshine Coast School District's *Spirit Canoe*, steered by Ed Hill, approaches at speed during the 2009 Pulling Together journey. A Métis sash adorns the bow.

A fleet of two-hatch baidarkas near Cook's Inlet in the Gulf of Alaska. This is an engraving from a sketch drawn aboard George Vancouver's ship during his voyage in 1794. COURTESY OF ROYAL BC MUSEUM, J-00196

left George Dyson's tree house, twenty-nine metres up in a Douglas Fir in Belcarra Park, in 1973. RON ORIEUX, COURTESY OF GEORGE DYSON

below Two children visit George Dyson in his tree house in 1975. The children were too small to climb from branch to branch and were pulled up by rope. PETER THOMAS, COURTESY OF GEORGE DYSON

The forty-eight-foot-long *Mount Fairweather* floats off Belcarra Park in July 1975. Later modifications included a different sailing rig, longer outriggers, and the removal of the plexiglass bubble hatch covers. GEORGE DYSON

The interior of the *Mount Fairweather* as it nears completion in 1975. The aluminum rib cage supports spruce floorboards and a translucent tight skin of fibreglass laminate. PETER THOMAS, COURTESY OF GEORGE DYSON

Three twenty-eight-foot, three-hatch baidarkas built by George Dyson under a sail in ocean swells north of Prince Rupert in August 1977. The removable fan-shaped sails could double as tents at night. GEORGE DYSON

The author's son, Matthew, plays in his whitewater kayak in the tidal flow, which can reach speeds of up to seventeen knots, at Skookumchuck Narrows on the Sunshine Coast. CHRISTIANE RANK

The Grand Hall of Canada's Museum of History has a ceiling with a "canoe within a canoe" pattern and walls supported by paddle-shaped pillars.

SANFORD OSLER

A sturgeon-nosed, or kootenay, canoe in the 1880s. This unusually shaped canoe is found in southeastern British Columbia and parts of Siberia.

COURTESY OF ROYAL BC MUSEUM, D-02701

on youth at risk. Although many of the trips have been on the lower Fraser River, they have also journeyed on Okanagan Lake, in the Strait of Georgia, and on the open ocean from Tofino to Port Alberni, often triggering a canoe revival in the areas traversed. There was even a parallel trip one summer near Peterborough, Ontario, but it was unsuccessful in terms of inspiring an annual event back east.

When I heard about these coastal trips in big canoes, I wanted to experience one first-hand. The Tribal Journeys were primarily for Aboriginal paddlers (or pullers, as they were called), but the Pulling Together trips had many non-Aboriginals, albeit mainly police officers. I learned that their 2010 route would overnight at Cates Park, a five-minute walk from my home, and that I could likely join a canoe if I was there in the morning, ready to go. That's how I found myself paddling through Burrard Inlet on a July day in the Abbotsford Police Department's canoe under the command of retired inspector John Davidson, a past organizer of these trips and current member of the VisionQuest Recovery Society's board.

The 2010 Pulling Together journey was a week-long ocean trip around the western part of Metro Vancouver, from Port Moody to White Rock. This was a new route for the group and coincided with the official naming of the waters travelled as being part of the Salish Sea, in recognition of the Coast Salish peoples' historic use of this waterway. For the first time, the journey was organized by a group other than a police force—the Aboriginal Youth Canoe Club operating out of Vancouver's Collingwood Neighbourhood House.

The fleet that morning consisted of about twenty big canoes, split evenly between voyageur and dugout style. All were fibreglass models until we were joined after an hour by the black cedar dugout canoe owned by the Squamish Nation that I had first seen at the salmon festival many years before. I was in a twenty-nine-foot voyageur-style canoe—one that James van Nostrand designed to fill the gap between the traditional North and Montreal canoes and that became Western Canoeing and Kayaking's most popular big canoe. Our route took us under both major bridges linking Vancouver and the North Shore. Normally, paddled canoes are not allowed in the busy waters between these bridges, but we had special permission and were escorted by harbour police and other police vessels—an arrangement that finally allowed me to paddle in the one stretch of local water that had been eluding me! We finished at the Welcome totem pole at Ambleside Beach to cheering crowds and official welcomes by the mayor and police chief of West Vancouver.

I learned there would likely be space for an experienced paddler later in the week for the long stretch from Steveston to Tsawwassen. This time I was assigned to *Skookum Kalitan*, meaning "strong arrow," the original thirty-one-foot RCMP Northern Dancer dugout-style canoe that had been on the 1997 VisionQuest trip and the first Pulling Together journeys in BC and Ontario. After travelling through Canoe Passage, we skirted the shallow Roberts Bank before being received by the Tsawwassen First Nation at the base of the spit to the ferry terminal. This stretch was the only one of the whole trip where we'd be on our own, as the escort vessels wouldn't be able to navigate the shallow waters (the coast guard's large hovercraft was supposed to cover this leg but was unavailable). It was the one stretch where we very nearly needed help.

The skipper of one of the big canoes had broken his long paddle that morning and replaced it with a regular-sized paddle, which was less effective at stabilizing the boat from his raised stern seat. This factor, combined with a seating change and simultaneous large wave, caused the canoe to take on water, first on one side and then the other. Fortunately, the swamped canoe remained upright while the paddlers emptied the water using extra bailers provided by neighbouring canoes. The skippers' radios crackled with the news, and we were all extra careful for the balance of that day. One of the paddlers on our canoe got sunstroke and was taken off as soon as the escort vessels were able to rejoin us.

I met three groups of people during the trip. The first were the officers from the RCMP and various Lower Mainland departments. Many were from Aboriginal policing units and were committed to the philosophy underlying the trip. One officer hadn't received permission from Ottawa to participate in the journey and so was doing it on her own time. They didn't match my preconception of a stern police officer; they represented the best of the new style of community policing. One officer told me that he wanted the youth to get a "natural high" from the experience.

The second group was the adults who weren't police officers. They often worked with troubled Aboriginal youth and included fisheries officers, teachers, and social workers. One of the people in my canoe ran the only recovery centre offering a residential program for addicted Aboriginal teenage girls from BC. Another was a social worker from a reserve in the Interior who had been involved in nominating youth for this journey.

The final group was the Aboriginal youth themselves. This trip was a big deal for them, some of whom weren't even teenagers. They had to train for weeks before the trip, get up very early some mornings after long evenings, and work hard during the day. Some dropped out before the trip started. My seatmate on the first day was a twelve-year-old boy whose parents had split up and were now living in Calgary and Vancouver, resulting in a rather disjointed life for him. Behind me sat two of the girls in the residential recovery program; they both hailed from communities with alarming statistics on youth substance abuse. My seatmate on the second day was a sixteen-year-old boy who was the eldest of six in a single-parent home on a reserve in the Interior. He was going into grade eleven and wanted to be a carpenter. I heard stories from various participants of how past trips had been transformative experiences, breaking down barriers between youth and police, and providing them with positive role models. Some of these kids wore T-shirts that read, "Canoeing Saved My Life . . . Ask Me How."

Some of the highlights for me of the Pulling Together experience were the evening programs. As we approached the beach bow first at the end of the paddling day, a spokesperson in our canoe would stand; introduce the canoe, stating where we were from; and seek permission to land from the local chief. Once permission was granted, we would back out, turn around, and land stern first, a sign of peaceful intent. I was especially happy that my sixteen-year-old seatmate got up the courage to be our spokesperson for the first time. We were then taken to the reserve's community hall or longhouse and treated like royalty, with an incredible feast featuring fresh seafood, as well as various ceremonies, dances, and speeches. I felt honoured to get a glimpse of this world and its traditions. I was particularly struck by the skill of the orators, the degree of gratitude shown to all involved, and the respect shown to elders. On the final day of the journey, everyone received something, and the gift giving went on for several hours. For the youth on the trip, it was a chance to get exposure to different cultures and customs, and to increase their sense of identity and heritage.

The stories of two young paddlers on the Pulling Together trips illustrate the impact the experience has had on them. Sixteen-year-old Katherine Hamilton from Port Alberni went on the journey reluctantly after she was caught fishing illegally and her parents got a call from the police department suggesting she join them on a paddle. It turned out to be a life-changing experience. In addition to getting her thinking about her education and career path, Katherine had the opportunity to paddle with the Lieutenant-Governor—and apparently made quite an impression on him! "He said I'm either going to be Prime Minister one day—or B.C.'s most wanted," she is quoted as saying in the *Globe and Mail*.[27]

Another youngster, Chantelle Desjarlais, was just fourteen when she went on her first of five Pulling Together journeys, even though she and her friends lacked their own support team or canoe. Saying that "this one canoe journey changed everything," she and her peers created the Kwu Sukwna'qinx Canoe Family organization and returned the following year with their own vessel. The youngsters' determination and ambition also translated into their academic lives. While high school dropout rates are high in some First Nations communities, Chantelle and every member of her original crew have graduated and some are now attending post-secondary institutions.[28]

One of the legacies of the canoe journeys that started with the 1997 VisionQuest is that the VisionQuest Recovery Society was able to open its first addiction recovery house in BC in 2004 and its world-class, stand-alone, ninth recovery facility in 2013, making it the single largest provider of supportive recovery in BC. Overseen by a board chaired by a retired assistant commissioner of the RCMP, the society serves over one hundred clients at any point in time who are all substance-addicted with criminal records, most coming straight from jail. The society employs an innovative abstinence-based model in a six-month intensive program offering a comprehensive healing journey involving mind, body, and spirit, and claims a recovery success rate three times the national average.

Another legacy is that Abbotsford's Western Canoeing and Kayaking continues to produce the modern fibreglass thirty-one-foot Northern Dancer and has sold over fifty of them to Pacific Coast communities from Oregon to Alaska, most of them for First Nations communities or organizations in BC. They subsequently added the southern-style twenty-four-foot Clan Dancer; thirty-six-foot Pacific Dancer; and another northern-styled canoe, the thirty-nine-foot Spirit Dancer—all based on the original ocean-going canoes of the Northwest Coast.

The availability of these relatively lightweight and low-maintenance craft in varying lengths and styles complemented the revival of the carving of dugout ocean-going canoes along the coast. Two of the most prolific carvers are Joe Martin in Tofino and Ray Natraoro in North Vancouver, both responsible for more than twenty dugout canoes, mainly ocean-going ones. Squamish Master Carver Natraoro began canoe carving in 1998, and his longest canoe is fifty-five feet. Once he finds the right old-growth tree, he hopes to build a sixty-five-foot canoe—a canoe that will be the longest dugout in use on the coast. He comes from seven generations of carvers and is grateful he can bring the spirit of a tree to life in a canoe using modern tools and traditional designs. This resurgence of the ocean-going canoes, both wooden and fibreglass, combined with the large number of longer voyageur-style canoes, makes BC the big-canoe capital of Canada, if not the world.

chapter three ——

THE SKIN CANOE

FARTHER north on the Pacific North American coast, another ocean-going craft was developed. Called *qayaq* in Inuktitut, loosely translated as "man-boat," it was a decked, skin-covered canoe. It was the lifeblood of those who lived in coastal areas where trees were small or non-existent.

In North America, kayaks ranged throughout the top of the continent, from the North Atlantic through the Arctic to the north Pacific Ocean. They came in varying lengths, widths, and designs depending on their purpose and the environment in which they operated. Generally, they were long, narrow craft with dehaired seal, sea lion, or caribou skins sewn together with natural thread, covering a skeleton made from wood, bone, and ivory. All the materials were locally available unless the drift-wood was inadequate, in which case long treks to below the treeline were required.

The prime purpose of the kayak was to hunt sea mammals, including seals, walruses, whales, narwhals, and sea otters. The Inuit also sometimes hunted caribou and sea birds from a kayak. Each vessel typically had an opening for one hunter, almost always a man. The hunters in their kayaks often worked in groups, for example, creating a circle around the last spot a seal surfaced or moving in a line to drive a whale into shallow water. Their primary weapon was a harpoon attached to a sealskin float, supplemented by one or more spears. The hunters generally propelled themselves with a double-bladed paddle, often inlaid with bone or ivory on the edge to protect the blades.

Kayak making was a critical skill as it enabled Inuit to hunt sea creatures in open water and hence allowed families and communities to survive. The skin of the prey, harvested from a kayak, yielded clothes and blankets for warmth, food for nutrition, and oil for light and heat. The animals also provided the material needed to re-cover the kayak every several years.

The kayak was modelled on the sea mammals it was used to hunt. The Inuit believed the hunter and hunted were equals in a shared and integrated environment and that the animals could be caught only when they were shown respect. Their spiritual beliefs are evident in these two comments by Inuit hunters:

> All the creatures that we have to kill and eat, all those that we have to strike down and destroy to make clothes for ourselves, have souls, like we have, souls that do not perish with the body, and which must therefore be propitiated lest they should revenge themselves on us for taking away their bodies.[1]

> Whaling is a sacred affair to the Inupiat hunter . . . The belief that spirits are embodied in sea mammals is very

strong among the northern Inuit . . . An appropriate
ceremony must be conducted when a whale is landed by
the whaling crew to avoid insult to the spirit of the whale
and other sea mammals.[2]

Although various types of kayaks were found across the top of this continent, the one most linked to British Columbia was the kind used along the southern Alaska coast and the Aleutian Islands. Now known as baidarkas, a term coined by the Russians, they were typically made from driftwood, whalebone, and sea lion skin and were particularly long and narrow; some could even carry more than one person. These were the ultimate travelling kayaks, able to go long distances at fast speeds as well as handle the open North Pacific. Paddlers learned to dip underwater (using what was later called the "Eskimo roll"—a full underwater rotation by a seated kayaker) to avoid heavy breaking waves. They kept dry by lacing the skirt of their watertight jackets to the manhole rim. Baidarkas were likely traded down the coast, as there is clear evidence of their presence at the time of first contact with Europeans along what is now the BC coast.

A distinguishing feature of the baidarkas was their bifid, or split bow, which may have served both figurative and functional purposes. John Jennings was particularly intrigued with the bifid, writing: "Symbolically, the two 'arms' of the split bow may symbolize an otter swimming on its back where the forward arm represents its head and the aft arm represents its front paws. Functionally, the two-part bow is an ingenious design that furnishes a sharp bottom surface for cutting the water and a larger upper surface for buoyancy."[3]

In their 1964 book, *The Bark Canoes and Skin Boats of North America*, Tappan Adney and Howard Chapelle wrote that the baidarka was "a more complicated and more developed instrument of the chase than is to be found in any other form of hunting canoe, due in part, perhaps, to the great craftsmanship of the Eskimo."[4]

Europeans came in contact with what they called a "skin canoe" as they sought to find a northern passage linking the Atlantic and the Pacific Oceans. Martin Frobisher, for example, in his voyages in the 1570s, reported being met by up to one hundred kayaks at a time as he sailed from the Atlantic side. Similarly, George Vancouver was met by many skin canoes as he approached Alaska on his way up the Pacific coast.

Excerpts from the diaries of early European visitors indicate they were clearly impressed by both the quality of the Native craft and the skill of the paddlers. A young lieutenant aboard ship in 1814 wrote:

> Alongside the ship, were paddling a large assemblage of canoes, of the most curious construction: these were built of a wooden frame-work of the lightest materials, covered with oiled seal-skin, with the hair scraped off; the skin being sewed over the frame with the most astonishing exactness, and as tight as parchment on the head of a drum. But the most surprising peculiarity of the canoes was their being twenty-two feet long, and only two feet wide. These canoes are only capable of containing one person, for any useful purpose; the slightest inclination of the body, on either side, will inevitably overturn them; yet in these frail barks will the Esquimaux smile at the roughest sea.[5]

A trading captain who had seen kayaks in 1656 noted:

> They are so confident in [kayaks], and so vers'd in the guiding of them, that they shew a thousand tricks in them . . . diving and rouling themselves in the Sea three or four times together; so that they may be taken for perfect Amphibia . . .[6]

Martin Sauer, sent by Russia's Catherine the Great to inspect her Alaska holdings, had this to say about Aleut seamanship:

> *The natives, observing our astonishment at their agility and skill, paddled in among the breakers, which reached to their breasts, and carried the baidarkas quite under water; sporting about more like amphibious animals than human beings.*[7]

Sauer also commented on the Unalaska kayaks:

> *If perfect symmetry, smoothness, and proportion, constitute beauty, [the kayaks] are beautiful; to me they appeared so beyond anything that I ever beheld. I have seen some of them as transparent as oiled paper, through which you could trace every formation of the inside, and the manner of the natives sitting in it; whose light dress, painted and plumed bonnet, together with his perfect ease and activity, added infinitely to its elegance.*[8]

George Dyson's 1997 book, *Baidarka: The Kayak*, also includes early European visitors' comments about the superior nature of the craft. In 1814, Georg Heinrich von Langsdorff wrote, "In my opinion, these baidarkas are the best means yet discovered by mankind to go from place to place."[9] And Russian Orthodox missionary Ivan Veniaminov, in 1840, enthused: "It seems to me that the Aleut baidarka is so superior in its kind, that even a mathematician could not add much if anything to its further perfection."[10]

Another European to visit northern Canada and the Bering Strait area was John MacGregor. He was inspired by the kayaks he saw and built a fifteen-foot wooden-decked canoe with a cockpit in the middle, which was powered by a double-bladed paddle and sail. MacGregor travelled throughout Europe in his canoe and wrote about his journey in *A Thousand Miles in the Rob Roy Canoe*, published in 1866. He went on to found the Royal Canoe Club in England, which marked the beginning of the popularization of canoeing and canoe racing as a sport, first in Europe and then in the US.

Other countries traditionally haven't placed as much emphasis on the distinction between canoes and kayaks as we're used to seeing in Canada (for example, the International Canoe Federation governs both canoe and kayak racing), and the term *canoe* is defined broadly in many international paddling circles to include both types of craft. Native North Americans also sometimes appear to blur the line between canoes and kayaks. In the Northwest, some groups used boats with kayak proportions—some of which had decking—that are often referred to as "kayak-form canoes." But among Native creators, there was a fundamental difference between a canoe and a kayak, despite any similarities in appearance. The First Nations bark canoe was built "outside-in," meaning that the bark was shaped first and the wooden structure was added inside later. In contrast, the Inuit kayak was built "inside-out": the skeletal structure was created first, and then the skin was attached to it.

Although the European visitors may have admired and copied the Inuit kayak, they generally didn't consciously seek to change it or control those who paddled it. The exception was the Russians, who saw the potential fortune to be made from using baidarkas to harvest sea otters for their thick fur coats. They began a deliberate policy of enslaving the Aleuts, enlarging the baidarkas and reaching farther afield in large fleets of kayaks. They scoured the Alaskan coastline in groups of up to eight hundred baidarkas and later reached as far as the Baja Peninsula and northern Japan in search of sea otters. As these mammals neared extinction and modern civilization increasingly encroached upon the Arctic, the building and use of skin kayaks declined.

I noted the scarcity of the craft first-hand when I worked in Canada's High Arctic during the summer of 1971. Based in Resolute, Northwest Territories (now Nunavut), a small community on an island on the northern shores of the Northwest Passage, I worked with a team of international scientists studying the ecosystem of a small nearby lake. (I was likely hired because I was one of the few people willing to dive under two metres of ice in the interest of science.) During my time off, I would sometimes visit the local Inuit community of about a hundred people, but I never saw a skin kayak, thinking at the time that its absence was due to the sorry history of Resolute.

In the 1950s, the federal government had relocated Inuit families from two less northerly communities to their newly created airstrip, weather station, and Royal Canadian Air Force base at Resolute in order to establish a larger presence in this strategically important area during the Cold War. Assured there would be good hunting in the new area, Inuit in fact found game resources scarce, and it was difficult for them to maintain a traditional lifestyle in the new location. The skin kayak essentially disappeared throughout the Arctic in the 1960s, and so it would have been difficult to find one anywhere at that time.

Around the same time I was in the Arctic, unable to find any skin boats, another young man was researching and trying to revive the baidarka, arguably the best of the Inuit kayaks. George Dyson was born in New York State in 1953, the son of Freeman Dyson, a leading theoretical physicist. The younger Dyson showed an early interest in boats and built his first kayak in his bedroom at age thirteen, a canvas-on-wood craft based on plans by well-known British canoeist Percy Blandford. When he was seventeen, Dyson moved to Vancouver, where his half-sister lived, and spent the next two years helping to build, and then working on, a forty-eight-foot ferroconcrete boat. One night Dyson and his shipmate hit a thirty-foot cedar log, which Dyson then towed into Vancouver harbour and converted into cedar shakes, some of which he sold and some of which he used in the construction of an unusual house.

Like the first Spanish explorers in the area who wrote in 1792 that "it would certainly be impossible to find a more delightful view,"[11] Dyson fell in love with Belcarra, a small area in Metro Vancouver on the east side of the glacial fjord Indian Arm. He so loved the view that he built a small house nearly thirty metres above the ground in a large Douglas fir at the edge of the ocean. He reached his cedar-clad six-by-six-foot tree house by climbing up the branches, raising supplies using a pulley system. Shared with flying squirrels and raccoons, his tiny house had panoramic views through five windows and was heated by a small wood-burning stove. This tree house was his home for three years, and Dyson prided himself on creating a dwelling that was both cheaper to build and higher than the one Henry David Thoreau had created more than a hundred years earlier.

Despite his integral association with a tree, Dyson had no interest in wooden or dugout canoes. Rather, he pursued his childhood interest in kayaks, studying various books on the baidarka and the Russian involvement with them. He was fascinated by the adventures of the Russian fur traders, describing them as "brutal men in a brutal time," but admitting, "yet my imagination was captured by the simplicity of their boats and the astounding magnitude of the voyages they had made."[12] He also believed that "modern kayak design paled in comparison with the designs of the Aleuts, whose vessels had evolved in imitation of the sea mammals out of whose skins and skeletons they were made."[13] He was determined to design and make his own modern version of these craft.

Building on an earlier one-hatch, sixteen-foot model he had constructed in 1970 using aluminum tubes, Dyson wanted to design a large kayak with the Russian-inspired three hatches. This time there were no drawings or diagrams of the original craft to guide him, so he had to innovate. The result was a sixty-eight-kilogram fibreglass-on-aluminum-tube boat with two sails and a rudder—the latter definitely being a new feature. Although small, the sails caused the kayak to climb half out of the water and plane in the right wind conditions, much to Dyson's surprise and delight. In the first summer he paddled and hitched a ride to Glacier Bay, Alaska, at the top of the Inside Passage. He returned the following spring and reversed the process, paddling and getting a ride back to Vancouver, after working with scientists in Alaska amid wolves, bears, and whales. He was back in his tree house to start work on his ultimate creation.

Perhaps influenced by his father's dream of building a spaceship the size of Chicago,[14] Dyson wanted to create a twelve-hatch, sixty-two-foot kayak. Unable to get funding for the venture, he settled on a six-hatch, forty-eight-foot craft, still the longest kayak ever built. Using the same fibreglass-on-aluminum-tube structure, it weighed over three hundred kilograms with its wooden floorboards and was called the *Mount Fairweather*. Describing his new creation, Dyson said, "It's totally new. It's a new kind of consciousness. If the spaceships come, and they want a specimen of intelligent life, this is what they'll take."[15]

Like Dyson, the mountain the kayak was named after is a dual citizen of Canada and the US, as it sits on the Alaska–BC border near Glacier Bay. It's the highest point in British Columbia. Describing the impact of the mountain on him, Dyson wrote:

Being near such a big mountain—"the paddler's mountain," the Tlingit had named it—had much to do with my decision to build so big a boat. The base of Mount Fairweather marked the region where the territories of the dugout canoe and the skin boat had overlapped. In my new project I sought to combine elements of both.[16]

Dyson continued to modify his creation as he got paddling experience in it. The kayak became a trimaran with the addition of two twenty-eight-foot outriggers, which improved stability and increased capacity through the use of platforms on either side. Most of the Plexiglas bubbles covering the hatches were replaced with flat covers, and the three small sails became one large one. But the distinctive dragon head at the bow remained.

Dyson described the *Mount Fairweather* as an unfinished chapter in his life because he never fully completed the boat.[17] Instead, he had a new vision of a fleet of baidarkas returning to the Northwest Coast, and he built six three-hatch, twenty-eight-foot "less interplanetary" boats. He hoped these kayaks, which he was able to live on for days at a time in an expedition to Alaska in 1977, would prove to be more practical and help keep the craft alive.

Dyson continued to scale down his designs, creating a two-hatch, twenty-four-foot kayak, and then a one-hatch, twenty-one-foot version in the 1980s. Not only were his designs becoming closer to the original Aleutian models, but so too was the material as he switched from the earlier fibreglass to a more skin-like nylon. As his biographer Kenneth Brower wrote in 1985, "George's baidarkas were evolving toward simplicity. His canoes had come full circle, strangely or not, and they were converging once again with the Aleut prototype."[18] Dyson also created kayak designs and kits, "to allow other twelve-year-olds—in age or spirit—to continue where I leave off."[19] He anticipated that the "design of these boats will adapt from generation to generation to meet the unforeseen, and to venture where no such craft has ever been."[20]

What motivated George Dyson to put so much time and energy into the renaissance of the baidarka? Kenneth Brower wasn't sure. Dyson told his father that his purpose in life was to clean up our sick and endangered world, in part by example.[21] He also said that he wanted to build the largest kayak in history to help revive canoe travel in BC and beyond.[22]

George Dyson is now credited with the revival of the baidarka style of kayak. Like Bill Reid, he carefully researched the past and built a modern version of a historic canoe for the first time in decades. But unlike the dugout canoe revival, the new baidarka did not spark strong interest among the descendants of the original builders and has not returned on the scale that Dyson probably would have liked. His most grandiose schemes, which included baidarkas two to three times larger than the *Mount Fairweather* that travelled the world, and solar wind sail–powered "space-kay-aks" traversing our solar system, have clearly not come to pass.

My own travels have overlapped those of George Dyson in several ways. In the same summer that Dyson was taking his first kayak trip up the Inside Passage to Juneau and beyond, I was on the *Northland Prince*, a passenger-carrying cargo ship that travelled from Vancouver to Prince Rupert, stopping at all hours to load and unload at coastal communities en route. From Prince Rupert, I then took the Alaska Marine Highway system ferry to Skagway, just north of Glacier Bay. Our paths came close again in 1976 when the *Mount Fairweather* was on display at Habitat Forum, which I attended several times as a student at UBC. Most recently I visited the Belcarra site, which is about a kilometre—as the canoe paddles—from where I now live on the west side of Indian Arm. In fact, Dyson used to paddle across to the mall I walk to in order to buy his groceries. Parts of the house in the tall tree that Dyson called home for three years are still visible, along with cedar shakes, Styrofoam, rope, and other remnants near the tree's base. Most interestingly, the *Mount Fairweather* rests on land nearby, along with its outriggers.

George Dyson moved from Belcarra to Bellingham, Washington, just across the international border, in 1989 and built a workshop on the oceanfront with the aim of producing kits so others could easily build their own baidarkas. He had begun that process and sold a few kits when he was approached to write a book on the evolution of digital computing, which led him to publish three books on various aspects of the history of technology over the next twenty years. He hopes to return to designing kayaks, particularly twenty-four-foot, three-hatch models, which he thinks would sell well. He remembers Belcarra as "as a remarkable place to live,"[23] providing a supportive and low-cost environment for him to explore and create.

—

At about the same time that George Dyson was starting to build ever-bigger kayaks, another young man in Vancouver was starting to build ever-more compact ones. As a child, Doug Simpson was also inspired by a British canvas-on-wood kayak—in his case while holidaying in Howe Sound, BC—and later saw the opportunity for a collapsible or folding kayak when he was flying in bush planes from lake to lake as a summer prospector in Canada's north. He too researched the traditional skin canoe designs documented by Howard Chapelle, co-author of *The Bark Canoes and Skin Boats of North America*, and he thought that a modern version could be made from the aluminum tubes used in small aircraft. Simpson started to work part-time on this vessel in a shack on Vancouver's Granville Island in the 1970s and now owns and operates Feathercraft, a designer and maker of folding kayaks that's still based on Granville Island.

Folding kayaks were first built in Germany in the early twentieth century and were popular in Europe in the 1920s. They were well suited for use on rivers such as the Danube, where, after being paddled downstream for the day, they could be collapsed and transported back by train or bus to their starting point. What Doug Simpson did was design and build folding kayaks for use on the ocean—high-performance craft that could be paddled for days at sea and then collapsed to fit the size and weight restrictions for a checked bag on airplanes.

Feathercraft now produces a dozen nylon-on-aluminum-tube collapsible kayaks ranging from a one-hatch, thirteen-foot model to a two-hatch, twenty-foot version. Most of the company's products are sold to customers outside Canada, particularly Japan. They have been paddled around the world, including the entire BC coast. Simpson himself has rounded Cape Horn and spent many days at sea travelling from Japan to Taiwan in one of them. Overnight trips are possible as the bulkhead-free bow section of the vessel can serve as a sleeping space.

Doug Simpson and George Dyson both followed the same basic design principles developed and refined for centuries by the Inuit. Doug Simpson was presented with the BC Creative Achievement Award of Distinction by Premier Gordon Campbell in 2010, "in recognition of extraordinary creative accomplishment in applied design . . . through the development of his world-renowned foldable kayaks."[24] His customers are clearly impressed with his kayaks as well. One wrote of paddling from Washington State to Alaska and then returning by plane, ferry, and bus with the kayak in his backpack. A ship's captain reported on his pleasure in being able to take his kayak on local buses and then paddle back to his 730-foot ship.[25]

When George Dyson and Doug Simpson were testing the limits of applying modern techniques to traditional Inuit kayak designs, others in Vancouver were starting to build kayaks closer in size and form to the originals. Ever since fibreglass was introduced to boat building in the late 1950s, committed individuals would build their own kayaks from an existing mould. In 1974, Steve Schleicher and his partner were building small kayaks for friends in a converted chicken coop behind his parents' house in Vancouver. They decided to design and build a larger version for the retail market, but it sat on display at Mountain Equipment Co-op all summer without a buyer. In 1975, Mike Neckar, convinced he could improve on the British-designed kayak, built eight for use on the ocean in a falling-down shop south of Whistler. Sales were slow, and ocean-going kayaks were scarce.

In 1980, on Granville Island, John Dowd opened the first North American store dedicated exclusively to a boat whose name he created. Previously known as "sea canoe" or "canoe tour," reflecting the British influence, Dowd coined the term "sea kayak" for the ocean-oriented boats he sold and wrote about. Meanwhile, Brian Henry, after a month-long paddling trip to Haida Gwaii in 1981, quit his job, opened a kayak store in Victoria, and started to design sea kayaks there. Shortly thereafter, Dowd organized a meeting that led to the creation of the Trade Association of Sea Kayaking (TASK), which laid the foundation for a viable sea kayak industry. He started *Sea Kayaker* magazine, and the sport began to enter the mainstream, aided by the introduction of plastic kayaks that sold for half the price of fibreglass ones. Schleicher, Neckar, and Henry, whose companies made Nimbus, Necky, and Current Designs kayaks, respectively, became leaders in the field, both in design and production methods. These companies continue to produce quality sea kayaks today, albeit under different ownership in some cases. Later BC entrants such as Atlantis in Ladysmith, Delta in

Maple Ridge, Lightspeed in Coombs, and Seaward in Chemainus, continued the tradition of producing fine sea kayaks. Slogans such as "the leading builder of premium kayaks in the world," "the ultimate kayaks for those who love kayaking," "the most technically advanced kayaks in the world," or simply "world's best kayaks" indicate the market positioning they seek. Beautiful cedar-strip sea kayaks are made to order, or sold as kits, by Coquitlam-based Orca Boats.

My own experience with sea kayaks began on Ontario's Georgian Bay in the 1980s. I'd heard about these new craft and wanted to try one. A kayak touring company was introducing it to people, and I took part and loved it. Later, in North Vancouver, my children both worked for the nearby Deep Cove Canoe and Kayak Centre, which hosts weekly paddling races. It also runs a large kayak rental operation, and my wife and I would take out the company's boats each summer to explore the local waters of Indian Arm. Our longest outing was when we and another couple rented double Seaward kayaks to circumnavigate Bowen Island in Howe Sound. The fastest competitors in the annual thirty-two-kilometre Round Bowen Challenge, North America's longest one-day kayak race, do it in under three hours, but we took two days, staying overnight at a bed and breakfast at the halfway point. It was a wonderful way to see the sometimes wild, sometimes developed shoreline of a beautiful island.

While clearly a leader in the design and manufacture of sea kayaks, BC has also helped advance the other extreme in kayaking—the short, one-person kayaks known as whitewater, river, or play boats. These kayaks were more popular than sea kayaks in the 1970s, inspired by their use in slalom races in the 1972 Olympics. When Nimbus's Steve Schleicher couldn't sell his early sea kayaks, he turned to designing and building whitewater kayaks, making important improvements in the materials and methods used to enhance both the toughness and durability of his boats. The advent of competing plastic whitewater kayaks, which were less expensive to make and easier to maintain, hurt his sales, but he refused to follow, concerned about their poorer performance. Instead, he redirected his attention to the sea kayak, which had a larger potential market and at that point was beginning its growth phase. Looking back, Scheicher said, "The goal was always to have a really neat way to travel in the wilderness, self-propelled. And that seems to be what most of our boats are actually geared to do."[26]

Necky's Mike Neckar, on the other hand, was a whitewater kayak champion, and he continued to design and build both whitewater and sea kayaks. Alternatively described as an industry legend, engineering genius, and magician,[27] Neckar led the revolution in whitewater kayaking in the 1990s when he introduced the Nimbus Jive, which had a flat planing hull and was a hit with beginner whitewater river- and ocean-surfing kayakers. My son had a Jive, which I've paddled. Whereas he used it as intended, in running rivers that canoes couldn't handle or for surfing on the open ocean, I paddled on local protected ocean waters to get a feel for it. A novel use of these short kayaks in our local waters is a game called "canoe polo." A combination of water polo, basketball, and kayaking, it's played by two teams of five people in kayaks. The winning team scores the most goals in the opponent's net. Paddling skills are important, and a good Eskimo roll is very valuable in avoiding an opponent. The sport has developed to the point where it has world championships organized by the International Canoe Federation.

Mike Neckar sold Necky to a large American company in 1999 but continues to live in Abbotsford designing kayaks through his new company, Delsyk Design Kayaks. One of his recent creations is a high-performance, easy-to-paddle plastic river-running slalom boat based on the one that earned a gold medal at the 2008 Beijing Olympics.

Making up the fastest-growing kayak market today are recreational craft. Usually between nine and twelve feet long, they fill a gap between the shorter whitewater kayaks and the longer touring kayaks, and are aimed at the recreational kayakers who are not particularly interested in speed or distance. One of the hottest sellers is Maple Ridge's Delta 10, which has a breakthrough design. Based on a modified catamaran hull, it combines speed, agility, and stability; it even comes with a window in the cockpit floor and convenient beverage holder. Recently, "coastal" kayaks between twelve and fifteen feet in length have appeared on the market and are proving popular. To support this growth in all types of kayaking, Surrey's Joe Matuska started Aqua-Bound in 1991 and soon became the number one producer of plastic-bladed kayak paddles, and the first to introduce injection-moulded paddle blades.

Interestingly, Western Canoeing and Kayaking has stayed out of designing and producing kayaks with one exception. They have, however, created the van Nostrand–designed Clipper Sea-1, a one-person, eighteen-foot canoe–kayak hybrid with a rudder and large cockpit that can be propelled with a single- or double-bladed paddle. This model was chosen by Joe O'Blenis for his successful six-thousand-kilometre solo trip from Kitimat to Montreal in 2004. Although he was followed by grizzly bears during the fifty-kilometre "Portage from Hell"[28] in BC, he arrived in Quebec uninjured and was very pleased with the Sea-1's performance. The lightweight Kevlar craft he used is also known for its speed and has won the Yukon River Quest, the world's longest annual canoe and kayak race.

I began to wonder why BC was such a leader in the design and creation of a variety of kayaks—large or small, for ocean and river, racing and recreation. There are no doubt a variety of reasons, but

I think one is the range of kayaking environments the province offers. Just as the Bowron Lakes Circuit is a world-class canoeing destination that attracts paddlers from near and far, BC has world-class kayaking sites. The Pacific Ocean, with its sheltered and exposed stretches, its islands and fjords, is a natural home for these craft.

For sea kayakers, one of the ultimate challenges is the circumnavigation of Vancouver Island, with its wild outer coast and more developed and congested inner coast. In fact, this twelve-hundred-kilometre route has become a hotly contested speed contest among the group of elite paddlers that like to do long, fast trips. Canadian Joe O'Blenis, who worked for Western Canoeing and Kayaking and now lives in Thunder Bay, regained the fastest solo kayaker title from a British paddler with a record time of sixteen days in 2010. This trip was no picnic with long days, painful blister-infested fingers, strong headwinds with breaking waves that capsized him once, and equipment problems that required a replacement kayak. The wildlife sightings were many and varied, though, and O'Blenis encountered hundreds of whales "to the point that you don't even turn around anymore when you hear them."[29] He used a traditionally designed kayak and paddle, and figures that if he did it again he could drop up to four days off his time.

For whitewater enthusiasts, it's hard to beat Skookumchuck Narrows, the choke point between Sechelt Inlet and the ocean on the Sunshine Coast. The daily tides cause predictable rapids, known as a tidal flow, of up to seventeen knots, second only to those in an isolated area of Norway. One enterprising group even offers to test new kayak designs, saying hours in these rapids are like years of regular use. This world-class tidal wave-riding opportunity in a provincial park is a huge draw along with other smaller tidal flow sites along the coast. BC's many rivers offer varying classes of moving water; Tamahi Rapids on the Chilliwack River, with its string of suspended slalom course gates, is a training site for the Canadian whitewater kayak team, and the site of many national whitewater championships.

———

Skin canoes, along with birchbark and dugout canoes, comprise the main canoe legacies that are alive and well in British Columbia today. They originated hundreds—possibly thousands—of years ago with Aboriginal people, and their design and methods of propulsion are remarkably unchanged, revealing the profound wisdom of these crafts' creators. Each type of canoe was incredibly well suited to its environment. For lakes, quick-flowing rivers, and gaps in between that required portaging, the canoes were lightweight and easy to repair. For oceans, including completely exposed areas, they were heavy and buoyant. And for a mixture of water, ice, and open-ocean conditions, they were small, nimble, enclosed vessels.

Much of this success could be attributed to the wealth of local natural resources available to the Native people—after all, birch and western red cedar trees provide excellent materials for canoe building. But the resourcefulness of the Inuit who built skin kayaks above the treeline in one of the world's most hostile environments using rudimentary tools and production methods truly amazes me. Not only were these craft functional, but they were also works of beauty. The lines, symmetry, and proportions are remarkable, and many of the exteriors were adorned with works of art.

What most impressed early European explorers, however, was the performance of these craft at the hands of a skilled crew. They witnessed paddlers run wild rivers, hunt massive whales far from sight of land, and roll underwater to avoid crashing ocean waves—skills essential for the survival of individuals and whole communities. It's not surprising that John Voss chose an old dugout canoe as the hull for his successful sailing trip around the world or that Europeans may have applied what they saw to improve their own ships. The owners of the *Titanic* urged their designers to get the right balance of strength and beauty in their massive new vessel. History suggests that Aboriginal canoes were more successful at achieving that balance.

The British Museum in London was designed to look like a Greek temple because ancient Greece was a much-admired civilization. In Gatineau, Quebec, at the Canadian Museum of History, the ceiling of the BC-focused Grand Hall is shaped like a canoe, and the supporting pillars are shaped like paddles—a fitting tribute to a craft that has meant so much to British Columbia.

chapter four

THE FIRST CANOES

AS I learned more about the rich history of the various forms of canoes in British Columbia, I regretted that I couldn't see and touch any of the ancient models. Because of the organic materials used in their construction, a canoe older than one hundred years is rare and usually isn't one that had been a working model. Imagine my surprise and delight, then, when I got the chance to see and touch a wooden canoe in good condition that was more than four thousand years old!

In June 2009, my wife and I visited the National Museum of Ireland in Dublin, whose archaeology collection features a fifty-foot oak dugout canoe in remarkable condition. The plaque said it was from the Early Bronze Age and had been dated from about 2,500 BC. This canoe had been found in 1902, buried in a bog near Galway on the west coast of Ireland by a farmer seeking peat moss to burn. The acid in the peat along with the lack of oxygen below the surface had created a near-perfect environment for preservation. Now the canoe is a star attraction in a national museum.

This chance encounter in Ireland started me thinking about how long people have been using canoes in British Columbia. That, in turn, led to the question of how long people had been in this province and where they came from. It has been accepted for some time that people had crossed from Eurasia to Alaska, perhaps taking advantage of a land bridge across the Bering Strait that resulted from the lower sea levels thousands of years ago. Indeed, I learned this theory in school: most of Canada had been covered in ice twenty thousand years ago, and it was only when an ice-free corridor was created east of the Rocky Mountains that the first humans had been able to enter this continent via a land bridge that then existed between current-day Siberia and Alaska.

This theory appears to be supported by recent genetic research. According to Dr. Tracey Pierre of the University of Cambridge, "all living Native Americans from North to South America belong to one of five lineages and can be traced back to southern Siberia."[1] Interestingly, two distinct historical connections between canoes and British Columbia reinforce this link with Siberia.

A little-known canoe found in the Kootenay and Columbia Rivers region of southeastern British Columbia is the Kootenay, or sturgeon-nosed, canoe, named because of its distinct bow and stern, which resemble the sturgeon fish that was once ubiquitous in the area. Ranging from ten to twenty-four feet in length, these canoes have a unique flat bottom, inwardly curling sides, and ends that slope downward and to sharp points just above the waterline. Traditionally made from white-pine bark over a cedar frame with small amounts of birch bark at the ends, they have also been made from spruce, balsam, or fir bark, and, more recently, canvas. The Ktunaxa Nation of this region characterizes white pine as "the tree that provides the bark for canoes."

The low pointed front on this canoe allowed it to cut through bulrushes in shallow marshy areas and facilitated paddling in strong winds. In addition, its elongated covered bow and stern provided valuable dry storage areas. In this mountainous region, canoes were the main means of transportation on lakes and rivers, and they were a means by which aquatic wildlife could be harvested. Explorer David Thompson recognized the uniqueness of this canoe's design as well as its suitability for that environment. And while unique to North America, the shape is strikingly similar to canoes found in the Amur River area of Siberia, providing further evidence of the origins of British Columbia's First Nations.

There are few bark sturgeon-nosed canoes remaining, and most of these are found in museums. Wayne Louie of the Ktunaxa Nation says every house used to have a sturgeon-nosed canoe. He is working to revive interest in this craft among his people by holding lectures and workshops and by building 2.5-, 5-, and 10-foot models, and occasionally bigger ones. In a 2012 conversation, Louie told me that according to the elders, the "Sturgeon-nose canoe is the keeper of our language, culture, heritage, history, and our identity . . . Without the canoe we're nothing."[2] Given how difficult it is to find white pines large enough to build authentic, full-sized sturgeon-nosed canoes, there is talk of using more modern materials to educate the youth about their canoe heritage.

The canoe also played a role in establishing a linguistic link between First Nations in British Columbia and Siberia. Professor Edward Vajda of Western Washington University presented a paper in 2008 following ten years of rigorous research that found the few remaining speakers of Ket, a native language spoken in Siberia, used almost identical words for "canoe" and "prow" to speakers of the Athapaskan or Na-Dene family of languages in western Canada.[3] This was the first-ever linguistic connection between the Old World and any First Nation in Canada and was recognized as a big breakthrough by other experts in historical linguistics. Interviewed about his discovery, Dr. Vajda said, "At that moment, I think I realized how an archeologist must feel who peers inside a freshly opened Egyptian tomb and witnesses what no one has seen for thousands of years."[4]

The current consensus about the last ice age on the northwest coast of North America is that the maximum period of glaciation, which resulted in virtually all of Canada being covered in ice, was from about 16,000 to 26,000 years ago. Sea levels were lower than they are today. As the weather warmed, glaciers melted and sea levels rose hundreds of metres, reaching above current levels 9,000 to 12,000 years ago. The degree to which the apparent sea level changed varied along the coast, depending upon the extent to which the earth's crust rebounded without the weight of the ice. Sea levels stabilized at their present height more than 5,000 years ago as temperatures rose to current norms and the rebounding stopped.

In the 1970s, archaeology professor Knut Fladmark at Simon Fraser University proposed an alternative to the prevailing ice-free corridor migration theory. He hypothesized that people migrated to the North American continent from Asia by travelling south by boat along the west coast. This thesis was inspired by new research that suggested plants had been growing along parts of the coast over eleven thousand years earlier, refuting conventional wisdom that the coast was still fully glaciated then. This research allowed for the possibility of an environment where people could have lived—an idea further supported by a 2012 study that found there were ice-free, people-friendly areas along the coast some seventeen thousand years ago.[5]

So what about these supposed people? Where was the evidence of early human life along the coast? Unfortunately, hard archaeological evidence has been difficult to come by, possibly because the rise in sea levels could have flooded any such sites near the ocean. But recent research on remains found in a cave on Haida Gwaii has confirmed through radiocarbon dating that people were there 12,600 years ago. According to anthropologist Quentin Mackie, this is the earliest archaeological site in all of British Columbia.

There is also good evidence of people living some thirteen to fifteen thousand years ago farther down the west coast of the continent on the US mainland and islands off its coast, and in Peru and Chile on the west coast of South America. The ice-free corridor could not have been the means of their arrival since it was not yet open. It is also considered highly unlikely that people were capable of crossing the full width of the Pacific Ocean at that time. Chilean geoarchaeologist Mario Pino Quivira goes even further: "If you take into account the technology available twelve to thirteen thousand years ago, [a twelve thousand–kilometre sea crossing] would be impossible. We know people just did not have enough sailing technology to cross such a long way from Australia to South America."[6] The evidence increasingly points to the possibility that the Americas were initially populated by people travelling down the west coast from present-day Alaska.

So how, according to this theory, did people move along the coast and get to islands like Haida Gwaii? As a student in the 1960s, Knut Fladmark had been told that Haida Gwaii (or the Queen Charlotte Islands, as they were then known) was probably uninhabited until about 2,500 years ago because the necessary boat-building capabilities wouldn't have existed. Yet there is now clear evidence that people were living on Haida Gwaii and other islands on the west coast more than twelve thousand years ago. It is tempting to suggest that cedar dugouts were the vessel of choice for these early island dwellers, but it has been established that cedar didn't begin growing in these areas until about five thousand years ago. All this is consistent with Haida oral history, with its stories of ancestors witnessing massive ice, a great flood, and the arrival of trees.

An important clue to how people may have travelled on the water at that time is a recently discovered, partially submerged site on Haida Gwaii dating back 10,700 years, which contains the remains of humans and sea mammals such as seals, otters, and sea lions. This confirmed for archaeologists that people were able to hunt and kill these ocean-based animals and must have been very skilled in a maritime environment much earlier than previously thought. It suggests that even with the lack of good trees, they were able to make and use boats. Mackie goes so far as to say: "The Haida are well-known as being one of the most marine-focused, marine-adapted, marine-fluent cultures in the world—anywhere, at any time."[7] Indeed, a 2008 article in the periodical *Science* stated, "The first Americans used boats, and the [Pacific] coastal corridor would have been the likely route of passage, since the interior corridor appears to have remained closed for at least another 1,000 years."[8]

But what craft would they have used to migrate along the coast? We know skin kayaks were generally made for only one person, had very limited cargo capacity, and were considered a "man's boat"; it was unlucky for a woman to paddle one. However, it turns out there was another skin boat, called an umiak, which complemented the kayak and may have been the key enabler of early coastal migration.

The original skin boat used by humans was probably a coracle, a small craft formed by stretching an animal skin over a round or oval frame made from branches. It was used in various parts of the world, including in China and elsewhere in Eurasia, and it may date back at least as far as forty thousand years ago, according to ethnologist Dr. Eugene Arima of the Canadian Museum of History.[9] At some point, it likely evolved to become

Wayne Louie of the Ktunaxa Nation holds one of the bark sturgeon-nosed canoes he makes near Creston. JOSIE AHEARN LOUIE, COURTESY OF WAYNE LOUIE

The umiak, shown circa 1904, is a large skin canoe that may have transported the first people to North America along the west coast over ten thousand years ago. FRANK H. NOWELL, COURTESY OF UNIVERSITY OF WASHINGTON LIBRARIES, SPECIAL COLLECTIONS, NA 2163

IN A 3-TON CANOE CARVED FROM A LOCAL DOUGLAS FIR LOG BY GEORGE B. TOCHER HE AND NAVIGATOR GERHARD KIESEL SAILED TO HAWAII FROM HERE 14TH. MAY, 1978, ARRIVING WAIKIKI 27TH. JULY, 1978

Plaque on Dundarave Pier in West Vancouver commemorating the voyage by the dugout canoe *Orenda* from West Vancouver to Hawaii in 1978. SANFORD OSLER

More than two months after leaving West Vancouver in May 1978, *Orenda* arrives off the coast of Hawaii. DOUG MCKAY, COURTESY OF RICHARD TOMKIES

Richard Tomkies lands the crew's first fresh meat in eighteen days. "Sushi sure beats canned beans and hard-tack!" he quipped.
GERHARD KIESEL,
COURTESY OF RICHARD TOMKIES

Orenda approaches Diamond Head in Hawaii. RICHARD TOMKIES

BC's Hugh Fisher and the Mohawk Nation's Alywn Morris receive their gold medal in two-man kayaking at the 1984 Olympics. Morris raises an eagle feather to honour all those who helped him achieve this result.
CROMBIE MCNIEL, COURTESY OF THE CANADIAN OLYMPIC TEAM

First Nations pullers compete in long, sleek Salish racing canoes at the Gorge in Victoria in 1903. CITY OF VANCOUVER ARCHIVES, IN P133

Mike Billy from the Squamish Nation with racing canoes he widened (*Mitzi* on left) or built (*Melanie* on right). SANFORD OSLER

Another view of *Mitzi* and three smaller Salish racing canoes at Cates park.
SANFORD OSLER

A fifty-foot Salish racing canoe in the eleven-woman race off Cates Park in 2010 (one man can paddle in the stern). SANFORD OSLER

Salish racing canoes compete in the eleven-man race off West Vancouver in 2013. This is a rerun of an earlier race in which all canoes swamped due to rough water. SANFORD OSLER

Vincent Lo putting the finishing touches on one of the larger dragon boats he designed and built. VINCENT LO

Four of the dragon boats built by Vincent Lo, complete with dragon heads and drums, ready to race at the big festival in False Creek in 2006. VINCENT LO

Women from Vancouver's False Creek Racing Canoe Club celebrate their 1995 gold medal victory in Hong Kong, making them five-time world champions in women's dragon boat racing. VINCENT LO

The original group of Vancouver women who bravely volunteered to test the value of upper body exercise after treatment for breast cancer. The success of the medical trial led to the formation of more than one hundred such dragon boat teams in a dozen countries. PHOTOGRAPHER UNKNOWN, COURTESY OF JANE FROST

A group of keen teens from Pemberton can't wait for the ice to thaw completely so they can practise for the dragon boat championships. DAVE STEERS, DAVE STEERS PHOTOGRAPHY

The Pemberton teens have to use a voyageur canoe in their practices since there are only two dragon boats available. DAVE STEERS, DAVE STEERS PHOTOGRAPHY

Pemberton dragon boat teams practise on the beautiful but tiny and water-lily-infested One Mile Lake. DAVE STEERS, DAVE STEERS PHOTOGRAPHY

Pemberton's Laoyam Eagles win the Junior Division at the 2013 Rio Tinto Alcan Dragon Boat Festival by a wide margin, the thirteenth straight year the team won at this major Vancouver event. KAREN TOMLINSON

Over one hundred paddlecraft, including some outrigger canoes in the fore-ground, gather at the start of the biweekly Big Chop race in Vancouver's English Bay in 2013. SANFORD OSLER

A birchbark canoe on the front of the Canadian dollar coin prior to the introduction of the loonie. SANFORD OSLER

Bill Reid's *The Spirit of Haida Gwaii*, also known as the *Jade Canoe*, is a popular gathering point at Vancouver International Airport. SANFORD OSLER

A white plaster version of *The Spirit of Haida Gwaii* sits in the Grand Hall of the Canadian Museum of History, and a dark version, known as the *Black Canoe*, rests outside the Canadian Embassy in Washington, DC.
SANFORD OSLER

Breast cancer survivors from eight countries, along with Vancouver steersperson Dr. Don McKenzie, paddle in the Diamond Jubilee Pageant on the Thames in 2012. PHOTOGRAPHER UNKNOWN, COURTESY OF JANE FROST

This sixty-five-foot canoe based in Prince Rupert is billed as the largest northern coastal First Nations canoe ever constructed and the largest canoe in North America. PAM MULLINS, PAM'S WILD IMAGES

Chris Cooper's forty-two-foot voyageur canoe *Spirit Dancer*, rigged with kayak outriggers in LeConte Bay, Alaska. CHRIS COOPER

A slimmer *Spirit Dancer* passes the cliffs of Dover en route from London to Scotland. CHRIS COOPER

Spirit Dancer reaches the Shetland Islands, well north of mainland Scotland, in the summer of 2013. CHRIS COOPER

Various types of canoes join the canoe gathering in front of Vancouver's BC Place to welcome the Truth and Reconciliation Commission to Vancouver in 2013. SANFORD OSLER

A group of canoes prepare to approach the welcoming stand prior to the Truth and Reconciliation Commission hearings. A spokesperson from each canoe will bring greetings to the officials. SANFORD OSLER

Skookum Kalitan and a collection of modern and traditional ocean-going canoes rest for the night. ED HILL

more seaworthy, with a distinct bow and stern, flatter bottom, and internal keel.

When Europeans began exploring the North American Arctic, they saw two types of skin boats in use: the kayak and the bigger, more comfortable, and more stable umiak. The umiak was an open boat made from walrus, seal, sea lion, or even polar bear split skins stretched over a sparse wooden frame. It was paddled like a canoe. A narrower version, which looked like a canoe, was used for whale and walrus hunting, while a wider version was used more for transporting people and goods. Although ranging from ten to sixty feet in length, umiaks were typically twenty to thirty feet long and could carry loads of up to five tons.

Umiaks were well designed for their environment. They were light enough to be transported over ice, yet strong and flexible enough to withstand being crushed by it. The skin and frame could absorb the shock of collisions with jagged ice, and rare tears could be repaired with blubber when necessary. Those in the Aleutians and southern Alaska were the most advanced; some had sealskin covers that could be raised to keep out spray, and sealskin floats that could be attached to the sides for additional seaworthiness. In the 1870s, Smithsonian ethnologist Edward W. Nelson noted that "with their boats fitted in this manner [the Inuit] sail fearlessly along their stormy coasts."[10]

The umiak impressed early European explorers. Captain Frederick Beechey of Britain's Royal Navy saw umiaks in 1826 in the Bering Strait and described them as "both light and pliable and very safe and durable."[11] In 1879, Swede Nils Nordenskiöld admiringly wrote that the Siberian umiak was "so light that four men can take it upon their shoulders and yet so roomy that thirty can be conveyed in it."[12]

Canadian Arctic photographer and author Fred Bruemmer went out in an umiak in 1975 on a long walrus hunt among the ice floes of the Bering Strait. His thirty-foot boat was made from five walrus skins, split to be one-inch thick, which had been carefully sewn together. He described the craft as "light, buoyant, strong and flexible," and "superbly safe and seaworthy."[13] He was impressed with the strength of the umiak and the skills of the nine-man crew. The Inuit consider the boat virtually unsinkable, something Bruemmer came to understand when one of the hunters shot a walrus through the bottom of the boat and simply patched up the hole with blubber. He felt that "in really dangerous conditions, the umiak has no equal," and said his crew's ancestors had been as famed as "Vikings of the Arctic Sea."[14] Roberts and Shackleton also admired this type of canoe as it "could withstand a buffeting from ice that would grind a European whaleboat to matchwood."[15]

On the critical issue of when and where the umiak was initially created, there is no hard evidence, although some suggest it predated the kayak. Arctic archaeologist William Laughlin made an "educated guess that it originated before the last ice age advance, perhaps in the Epigravittian period about the thirteenth century BCE in eastern Asia in the Sea of Okhotsk region."[16] This means the umiak may have first appeared about fifteen thousand years ago in the body of water just west of the Bering Sea, which separates Russia from Alaska. It may have been an elongated version of the age-old coracle found in that region.[17] Most significantly, the umiak may have been the craft that enabled the first men and women to travel from northern Eurasia down the west coast of North America and populate the Americas before other access routes were feasible. Anthropologist Dorothy Jean Ray writes, "After the umiak was invented, the [Bering] Strait became an intercontinental highway, its coastal fringes occupied by peoples who had more or less the same way of life . . . The Eskimo umiak has proved its superiority over all other boats [in the Arctic] time and again."[18]

The umiak may have also influenced the development of ocean-going canoes along the west coast of British Columbia. Roberts and Shackleton state this clearly when talking about canoes found on the west coast of Vancouver Island:

> Similarities between the Nootkan canoe and the skin-made hunting umiaks of the Bering Sea Eskimos and their Asiatic neighbors, the Chukchi, suggest that the umiak might be the parent of the southern dugout. Each craft has a flat bottom, flaring sides, and an almost vertical stern. Both were used for whaling with similar hunting equipment and a similar distribution of duties among the crew. The two societies preserved the same whale-hunting rituals, built a similar harpoon rest at the bow, and painted a similar sea monster on the side of the vessel. Even more convincing, old Nootka dugouts had scratch marks at bow and stern, painted on or grooved into the wood, conforming to the position of the lashings of an umiak. Along the inside of the old Nootka canoes is a wavy, painted line which is reminiscent of the edge of the umiak skin covering where it is rolled over the gunwale and laced down at intervals to the frame.[19]

It is unfortunate that the umiak, such an important type of canoe, is relatively unknown today. When the Russians occupied the Aleutian Islands and harnessed the men to hunt sea otters in their kayaks, they confiscated or destroyed the umiaks so that there was no way the families could escape or launch an attack against their occupiers. Later, changing technology meant that umiaks were gradually replaced throughout the Arctic with canvas freighter canoes or wooden boats with outboard motors. But there are still areas of northwestern Alaska and northeastern Siberia where traditional umiaks are preferred to noisier, heavier, tippier, and more puncture-prone modern boats that are used to hunt whales, particularly the bowhead.

I have never seen an umiak outside of a museum. I have, however, seen a crude seaworthy descendant of the coracle. After discovering the four thousand-year-old dugout canoe in Dublin in 2009, we went to the west coast of Ireland and found an Irish currach, also called a canoe in some of parts of that country. The currachs we saw were ocean-going boats made with tar-coated canvas stretched over a wooden frame. In the past, they were typically sheathed in animal skin or hide, usually from a cow, and were used in the Atlantic Ocean. Today they are also involved in racing, often doing well against more modern boats.

It should be noted that while the theory of the first humans coming to the west coast by boat is gaining acceptance by experts, there are skeptics. Anthropologist David Meltzer was quoted as saying:

> I've got a hard time with boats and refugia [human-friendly areas]. You have huge chunks of ice, hundreds of metres high . . . coming straight down and calving into the ocean. And there are a whole bunch of them. What's going to grow into these glaciers? Are you going to have cute little 7-Elevens where you go and get your 'Big Gulp' and make your way down south?[20]

We know that people in umiaks and kayaks were adept at hunting whales and other sea animals for food, but a paper published in 2007 suggests another source of food. The "Kelp Highway Hypothesis"[21] posits that the original colonizers of the American continents arrived by boat following the kelp forests of the Pacific Rim. These forests, which stretched along the entire west coast of the Americas except in the tropics, would have provided algae, seaweed, fish, birds, and other nutritional sources in relatively shallow waters for people migrating down the coast.

Kelp is not as plentiful today off the BC coast as it once was; the elimination of sea otters by European-inspired overhunting allowed the population of sea urchins to grow, which, in turn, inhibited the development of kelp forests through the destruction of the structures they anchored to.

Recent discoveries tend to further support the early arrival of people by boat. Genetic testing has found a very rare type of DNA in human remains in various locations on the west coast from South Alaska to the tip of South America. Dr. John Johnson, curator of anthropology at the Santa Barbara Museum of Natural History, has concluded, "This is the best evidence to date that there was a coastal migration leaving behind these pockets of people all along the western margin of the two continents."[22] And projectile points recently discovered in Oregon caves are at least as old as the oldest ones unearthed farther inland and, significantly, they are of a different style and created using different technology.[23] This further supports the view that there were different migration routes to America, with the coastal route likely being the first.

So perhaps now we the have key pieces of evidence to validate Knut Fladmark's coastal migration theory:

- Ice-free, plant-growing areas along the northwest coast some seventeen thousand years ago
- Human remains on Haida Gwaii from at least 12,600 years ago and farther south on islands and the mainland up to fifteen thousand years ago
- Very rare DNA found in ancient human remains at various points along the west coast of North and South America
- Haida Gwaii inhabitants' ability to hunt and kill sea mammals at least 10,700 years ago
- The likely availability in this era of skin boats used for hunting and for transporting women, children, and belongings to new areas

- The likely availability of rich and diverse kelp forests along the entire coastline outside of the tropics

Not only does migration by boat along the coast seem likely, but evidence suggests that it also pre-dated any other means of arrival. Archaeological remains show human existence along the coast before the ice-free corridor on the other side of the Rocky Mountains was open to human passage, or before the capability existed to cross the twelve thousand–kilometre expanse of the Pacific Ocean. Knut Fladmark's theory, once viewed with skepticism, is now the explanation most experts appear to believe. As Fladmark himself said, "If the coastal migration route hypotheses is correct, then Haida Gwaii may well have been the first part of modern Canada to hear human voices."[24]

—

Another theory involving BC and ancient canoe travel to new lands was proposed by Norwegian ethnographer Thor Heyerdahl in the mid-1900s. Heyerdahl argued that several thousand years ago, Asians from the Taiwan area travelled with the wind on the North Pacific current to the BC coast, settling in locations from Vancouver Island to Haida Gwaii and perhaps farther north. Then, about a thousand years ago, some of these people went by seagoing canoes to Hawaii and perhaps later to other Polynesian islands. He and his followers list a number of specific similarities between the material cultures of the BC coast and the South Pacific, including large ocean-going canoes, stone and bone pounders, war clubs, fish hooks and harpoon heads, large totem poles and other carvings, language pronunciations, and the non-use of pottery. They also note the ocean currents and trade winds that would support such a journey.

This theory is not widely accepted by today's experts, although a recent DNA linkage between Polynesia and the northwest coast strengthen the case. Some experts think an initial movement from Hawaii to BC is more likely than the reverse. More hard archaeological or genetic evidence will be needed to resolve this issue to the satisfaction of the academic authorities.

One man who believed in Heyerdahl's trans-Pacific migration theory and wanted to demonstrate it to the world was Geordie Tocher. Geordie's father, known as the "Wild Man of the North," was famous for making a nine-month trek through the mountains from Edmonton to Prince Rupert in the winter of 1920–21. Geordie inherited his father's sense of adventure. He worked as a high-rigger logger and whitewater rafting guide, among other things. He enjoyed skydiving, deep-sea diving, and flying planes for recreation, but his biggest dream was to travel by canoe from BC to Hawaii.

His first attempt in a fifty-foot cedar dugout canoe of his own creation ended in disaster on a reef off the coast of San Francisco. For his second attempt, he took almost three years to carve a forty-two-foot canoe from a three hundred–foot-tall Douglas fir that was between six hundred and eight hundred years old. The municipality of West Vancouver offered him the tree free of charge—if he felled it himself. He then added a seventeen-foot cedar outrigger for stability, two masts for sails, and three coverings for shelter. Tocher, age fifty-one; Karin Lind, his girlfriend; and Gerhard Kiesel, a veteran sailor, set off from West Vancouver in *Orenda*, a Haida-style dugout canoe, in May 1978. The first leg took them down to just south of San Francisco, where Lind left the canoe and Richard Tomkies replaced her. They then departed on the six-thousand-kilometre journey to Honolulu, following "the natural flotation path of logs and of the winds," and running into more than their share of bad weather and thirty-five-foot waves. Faulty radio equipment kept their progress unknown to the world until they arrived in Hawaii four weeks later. Tocher had established the feasibility of taking a dugout canoe on such a journey, and a plaque at the end of the Dundarave Pier in West Vancouver commemorates his adventure.

This much about the voyage of the *Orenda* I learned from newspaper articles, but I wanted to know more. Both Tocher and Kiesel are now dead, but Tomkies is alive and well and living on BC's Sunshine Coast. In our conversation, he confirmed that 1978 had been a bad year for storms; there were hurricanes in the Pacific, and twenty-knot trade winds created gigantic swells during their journey: "They weren't white caps; they were white cliffs. Sometimes you would have to look up sixty degrees to see the top of the wave." He told me of the canoe being hit once by a huge breaking wave that smashed their steering oar, disassembled the outrigger, and filled the boat with water. On another occasion, when on watch alone in the middle of the night, he heard this growing strange noise ahead; it turned out to be rollers crashing in the shallow waters off the island of Maui, which they narrowly missed.

Tomkies reported that the canoe performed well, and it definitely would have been possible for First Nations mariners to have taken the same trip from the BC coast thousands of years ago. They had little control over their course, but the trade winds and current took them naturally all the way to Hawaii. He believed the outrigger was essential; it enabled them to sail in the absence of a keel since progress by paddling alone would have been too slow in light of the amount of provisions the boat could carry. He felt the Native tradition of connecting two canoes would have served the same purpose. He remembered being very warmly received by native Hawaiians, who believed they were descended from BC First Nations. He said it would have been possible to return to BC by sailing canoe, but it would have been a much longer trip given the flow of the winds and current.

Having had no previous open-ocean experience, Tomkies found the setting "awe inspiring," making one feel "infinitesimal, like you are nothing." He remembers vividly the sense of sitting eighteen inches above an opaque surface of indigo blue and the "smell as big as an ocean" when they cracked open the bottle of champagne upon sighting land again. He also remembers not being able to initially walk on land, and in fact falling over after twenty-nine days at sea. Looking back, "he wouldn't have missed it for anything . . . it was a great trip." The reception back in BC was much more muted than that in Hawaii, and nothing more than a few newspaper articles has ever been published about the trip.

Unlike some earlier civilizations whose use of stone and metal makes it relatively easy to date their periods of existence, people using wood and skin left fewer long-lasting traces. This is particularly true when these people lived near an ocean whose levels have changed significantly during the course of human existence. Nevertheless, the sturgeon-nosed canoe found in southeastern BC suggests a distant link to native craft in Siberia, and various canoes and other clues hint at a possible link between Native people in BC and Polynesia, including Hawaii. An increasingly strong set of indicators suggest the very first people to arrive in the Americas did so by boat on the North Pacific. We speak today of BC being the gateway to Asia, but the BC coast was probably the original gateway to the Americas, courtesy of the canoe.

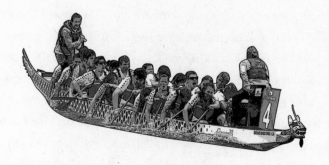

chapter five ——

RACING CANOES

MY first real exposure to elite-level canoe racing came at my niece's wedding in Mexico in late 2012. The groom was Mike Russell, a former member of the Canadian national canoe-kayak team, and one of the guests was Adam van Koeverden, fresh from earning his fourth Olympic paddling medal and being named Canadian male athlete of the year by the True Sport Foundation. Several other guests at the wedding were members of the close-knit community of Canadian canoe-kayak racing, and I couldn't resist asking them about their chosen discipline.

Unlike the other canoes that have been covered in this book thus far, which were originally designed for work (transportation, exploration, and trade), racing canoes are built for sport. Historically, in the record books, and still in some European countries, the two types of boats used in canoe racing are called "Canadian" (C) and "kayak" (K) canoes. Nowadays, they are typically referred to simply as canoes and kayaks. The Canadian canoe is open, and it is based on the original birchbark design. Appropriately enough, Canada's Frank Amyot won a gold medal in a "Canadian" canoe at the 1936 Olympics. It was the first year canoe racing was recognized as an Olympic sport, and it provided our only gold medal at those games. A pair of Canadians took silver and bronze medals in two-man Canadian canoe races that year as well.

Over the years, the boats evolved, and the Canadian canoes were redesigned by Europeans to become sleeker racing machines. The "C" in Canadian began to unofficially stand for canoe, but the craft continued to be paddled with one knee up, using a single-bladed paddle, in contrast to the fully seated position using a double-bladed paddle employed in a kayak.

Canoe racing in Canada has been governed by CanoeKayak Canada since 1900. Although nominally a national organization, its scope was initially limited to Ontario and Quebec; BC's involvement and influence was slow to develop. Of the twenty-four Olympic medals that have been won by Canada since 1936 in canoe-kayak events, only two were associated with BC. In fact, only one BC paddler has won a medal at the Olympics—Hugh Fisher. Paired with Alwyn Morris from Quebec in kayak doubles, Fisher won a gold and a bronze medal in 1984. Morris was the first, and still the only, Aboriginal Canadian to win a gold medal in the Olympics. When training at the Burnaby Lake race course prior to the Games, Morris, a member of the Mohawk Nation, would speak in his native language to a bald eagle that often perched atop the poles that marked the course. Standing on the Olympic podium, he raised an eagle feather to honour all those who had helped him achieve his dream. He used his resulting profile to become a role model for other First Nations people and helped promote the National Native Alcohol and Drug Abuse Program.

Hugh Fisher was raised in Burnaby, BC, and got hooked on paddling during a family canoe trip around the Bowron Lakes when he was in his early teens. He took up sprint kayaking on nearby Burnaby Lake in the centre of Metro Vancouver and watched it transform into one of the best paddling courses in the world for the 1973 Canada Games. He started to practise on the lake using the world-class canoes and kayaks acquired for the Games and with some of the top Canadian paddlers and coaches who were drawn to this facility. Fisher went on to found the False Creek Racing Canoe Club in 1985 to provide a downtown Vancouver training location. He remains the only BC person to have ever won an Olympic medal in sprint canoe-kayaking.

Nevertheless, BC has played an important role in helping Canadians from other provinces perform at their best. Fisher was able to attract some of the top coaches and kayakers in the country to train at Burnaby Lake, and this continued into the early 1990s, long after he retired from Olympic-level racing. The combination of a great training course on a centrally located, quiet lake that seldom froze over, along with good local universities for the athletes to attend, made it an attractive national focal point. With time, however, the athletes started to stay at or near their home clubs, most of which were in eastern Canada. From 1997 until 2008, there weren't even enough young people in the sport for it to be represented at the BC Summer Games. In 2010, the president of CanoeKayak BC said, "We still struggle as a Province to be represented significantly on the National Teams, which is sadly reflective of our impact as a sport on the local scene."[1]

I was curious as to why BC had not developed more top sprint canoe-kayakers despite the province's natural advantages and world-class training facilities. In the traditional sprint canoe-kayaking strongholds of Ontario and Nova Scotia, it's not uncommon to find families who have been involved in the sport for generations, which leads to higher enrolment among children and more long-term involvement. In addition, there are more clubs in close proximity to each another, offering more opportunities for competition. In BC, youth seem to be less motivated to take up the sport, or give up before they reach elite status. Perhaps there are simply too many options here, both on and off the water, for outdoor-oriented youth.

Sprint canoe-kayaking is starting to make a comeback in the province, with youth participation reintroduced in the 2010 BC Summer Games and some presence at the national level. Burnaby Lake was recently dredged to counter the ever-encroaching green growth and bring it back to its former quality as a training course, but serious athletes continue to leave the province to train elsewhere.

—

While the sprint canoes and kayaks used in the Olympics may not be catching on as widely here as in other provinces, there are other forms of racing canoes in which BC is a leader. When we first moved to North Vancouver, I saw a canoe called *Checkerboard* on display at Cates Park. It was built in the 1920s by Chief Henry George of the local Tsleil-Waututh Nation. The canoe, about fifty feet long and very narrow, held eleven people and was described as having won many Indian-war-canoe races. I had never seen a canoe like this before and began to research the background of the craft.

In the latter part of the nineteenth century, the Coast Salish people competed in regular summer canoe races. These were public events; indeed Canada's Governor General and his wife observed these races in Victoria and Alert Bay in 1876. The canoes used were the large ocean-going craft that were prevalent in those days. As these big canoes became scarcer, and as racers sought greater speed, their shape evolved to become even longer and narrower. Some say this shift in design triggered a revival of the long, narrow "war canoe," which the Salish nations used as scouting craft to detect hostile big canoes and then raced ahead to alert their people. In any case, the name "war canoe" stuck.[2] The races became popular spectator events in the 1930s, with some drawing thousands of people at different locations in the Salish Sea area. But they also served another important purpose. When the Indian Act banned potlatches in 1884, it became illegal for Native people to gather in large numbers for special events; however, getting together for sporting events such as these canoe races was legal, so the races continued as a way for nations to meet and keep traditions alive.

Despite its relatively small size, the Tsleil-Waututh Nation won canoe-racing championships from the 1930s to the 1970s. Their success began with *Checkerboard*, later rebuilt and renamed *Burrard View*, but it did not end there. In 1960, Chief Dan George built the eleven-person *Maria Legionis*, which proceeded to win a number of races in the 1960s. One of the paddlers, or pullers as they were known, in that canoe was a young Stanley "Spin" Thomas, who remembered those days with great fondness when I interviewed him at his home on the reserve.

Thomas said that canoe racing was the best sport around. In fact, it was the only inter-nation sport at that time. The season would begin right after Easter Sunday and finish with the final race on Father's Day at the Lummi Reserve in Washington. During that time, the paddlers were expected to follow a strict regimen of getting to bed early and having no alcohol, cigarettes, fried foods, or sex. I challenged him on the last point and he assured me there was a dip in the birth rate nine months following the season and a subsequent spiking of "canoe season" babies. He said they trained after school or work every day in the large canoe, and often in the early morning in smaller canoes. At the beginning of the season, they would sometimes end up *in* the water, but as they perfected their technique, the practices would get drier. The final selection of team members was based on time trials in single canoes.

Thomas reported that the races, which followed a circuit that included Cultus Lake, Vancouver Island, and Washington State, often attracted over thirty of these large eleven-person canoes. He put up with the gruelling training routine to keep their nations' tradition of success alive: "I wanted to call myself a winner like my brothers and uncles did, and to be a champion."[3] He said canoeing was his main source of happiness at that time; his personal highlight was winning Vancouver's annual Sea Festival and receiving the fifty-dollar prize awarded to each paddler in the victorious *Maria Legionis*. He attributes the team's success to the canoe (carved from a Stanley Park cedar with sides two centimetres thick and "light as a feather"), the man in the stern ("best coach of any canoe club around"), the two men at the front (who were consistently winning in singles and doubles races), and the weight of the paddlers (no one weighed more than eighty kilograms).

Stan Greene, another former paddler in the Coast Salish canoes, emphasized the importance of having the right attitude:

> *To get into a canoe, you have to be a proper person, a clean person in both body and mind . . . Don't be swearing around that canoe, don't be saying bad things. You're going to hurt that canoe's spirit and it won't go for you . . . I tell people you can be the strongest team on the water, but you have to have everything going for you—mind, body, and spirit. One of the main teachings of our people is to be a good person.*[4]

Participation by the Tsleil-Waututh and some other nations began to dwindle after the 1960s as soccer and other inter-nation sports were introduced. The larger, neighbouring Squamish Nation continued its interest in the discipline and even purchased a large racing canoe from the Tsleil-Waututh, whose canoe-building skills were widely admired. A young Mike Billy, a hereditary chief whose ancestral name, lem xacha Siem, means "canoe maker," began racing in the 1970s and was then introduced to the family tradition of carving dugout canoes. One of the first canoes that he became known for was *Melanie*, a very narrow twenty-six-inch-wide, six-person cedar dugout that was four years in the making and in which he won many big races. Another was the rebuilt *Mitzi*, a thirty-year-old dugout canoe made by his father that was too long to be a good two-person canoe but too narrow to hold four. Its odd dimensions resulted in *Mitzi* being underused, and long cracks and other forms of deterioration set in.

In an interview with me, Billy described the risky task of cutting the craft in half longitudinally in order to widen it enough to accommodate four people:

> *I sat by* Mitzi *with my coffee for about forty minutes and imagined that she felt scared, being stored up there for thirty years and never being used and always been a failure. I told her what I was going to do, that I had built canoes my whole life . . . and if there's anyone that can do this it's me. "And once I finish you, you're going to go to the races, you're going to win, you're going to be the best, people will tell stories and sing songs about you . . . you're going to be the greatest if you just trust me" . . . After I did it, no one could beat her. People are just amazed when they ride her; she's a legend now.*[5]

Billy continued to be an innovator in canoe design, striving to increase the speed of his boats. He was one of the first to introduce strip canoes, ones made with cedar lattice boards running parallel to the gunwales and held together with a fibreglass cloth, which were half the weight of those carved from a log. He later made fibreglass canoes moulded from a fast dugout canoe his brother had built. He's thinking of making racing canoes from even lighter materials in the future. Each time he introduced a faster canoe based on new methods, there was controversy about whether they should be allowed in races. His grandfather assured him it was fine to do anything to make a faster canoe and the innovations he introduced eventually became more common and accepted.

To Billy, making and racing canoes is everything. It's what he does and loves: "Once we're out paddling on the ocean and the sun is shining, it's like we're kings, we have the whole universe. We're becoming one with the ocean, the biggest thing on the planet . . . it's an amazing feeling that you can't reproduce. I wouldn't trade canoe racing for anything."[6] He took me out on one of those beautiful sunny days, and I think I understood how he felt. We were in a double strip canoe that his daughter had helped him build after she gave away her solo dugout at her grandfather's big potlatch. She had asked her father for a fast, easy-to-steer canoe with an original design that he created "from the numbers in [his] head." The design proved to be both successful and popular. Billy called it his Cadillac design, and it was certainly more stable than I had expected.

The Tsleil-Waututh Nation resumed hosting regular canoe races at Cates Park in 2010. In July of that year, I witnessed more than a dozen of these narrow fifty-foot canoes, as well as many shorter ones, as part of a two-day racing event there. Today, First Nations canoe races are held at different locations in southern BC and northern Washington virtually every weekend from May until August. The canoes hold one, two, six, and eleven paddlers, with race categories for men, women ("klootchmen"), family, elders, and children ("junior bucks" and "buckskins"). Both dugout and strip canoes compete in the same races for the same cash prizes, and some fast children are thrilled to win over $100 in a weekend.

The races at Cates Park are quite a sight to behold, with canoes bearing names such as *Island Brave*, *Ocean Thunder*, *Savage 11*, and *Ultimate Warrior*. Tsleil-Waututh chief Justin George, grandson of canoe carver Chief Dan George, welcomes all the racers, writing: "Canoe-pulling is a celebration of our connection with the rivers and the ocean in our territory. It also honours the trade and diplomatic relations we have with our First Nation neighbors. The canoe embodies discipline, respect, teamwork and unity."[7] Former canoeing champion Ernie "Iggy" George briefs the skippers on the course and race rules. They start in groups of up to ten and race for as long as twenty minutes at a pace that can exceed eighty strokes per minute, switching sides in unison from time to time. The course is usually a circuit, with the boats finishing where they started. The narrowness of the canoes, waves from passing boats, and course manoeuvring can and do cause tipping and swamping. I spent some time with a family from Neah Bay, Washington, who travel in their RV to most of these races throughout the summer. They felt it was a great family activity and "kept the kids out of trouble."

On a July Saturday in 2013, I was sailing off West Vancouver and encountered conditions so rough that several of my passengers were seasick. My son later reported that the conditions had provided some of the best windsurfing in years. When I attended the Salish canoe races at the somewhat exposed Ambleside Beach area of West Vancouver the next day, I learned that Saturday's rough conditions had had quite an impact on the races. The early ones had been cancelled, but the signature event, the men's eleven race, proceeded. For the first time in anyone's memory, all eight of the racing canoes swamped, and one dugout canoe actually broke apart when the bow and stern straddled a wave. No further races were held that day, and even on the somewhat calmer Sunday, the racers in the bigger canoes had to dedicate two paddlers to bailing out the water that was coming in over the sides.

Although these racing canoes are found only in the Salish Sea area of coastal southern BC and northern Washington, aspiring Native youth can compete more broadly in the recently created BC Aboriginal Provincial Canoe and Kayak Championships using marathon canoes. Marathon canoes are a cross between the birchbark and Salish racing canoes, with long narrow bows but a relatively wide beam to accommodate the official racing specifications. The youth can also compete in the North American Indigenous Games in similar craft. Although the marathon canoes are more popular in the east, CanoeKayak BC is now helping interested Aboriginal youth train and compete in them in this province.

———

In 2002, I decided to get involved in another type of canoe racing that was gaining popularity in BC—dragon boating. I joined a new community dragon boat team based in Deep Cove after seeing an advertisement and went to my first practice that spring. Before long, the team had grown to over twenty members, all new to the sport, and we were practising two to three times a week. As we became more comfortable with the basics of stroke mechanics, learned about teamwork, and improved our physical condition, we would go farther afield and work on racing skills under the guidance of our experienced coach.

I really enjoyed these outings. It was a chance to get outside after the long wet winter and paddle in a fjord bordered by snow-capped mountains. As it turned out, I was the only man coming to the practices and one of the few people with any previous paddling experience. I learned that dragon boat paddle strokes were shorter than what I was used to, and that well-synchronized timing was more important than power. In additional to paddling, I was often the steersperson, the one who stood at the stern and steered the boat using a long oar leveraged on a vertical post. As the season went on, the coach, who sat in the front facing the paddlers, let me decide on the routes we took, and I had fun piloting our boat to different areas. I left the team as the race season approached, and they went on to enter women's events at several competitions in the province.

Although relatively new to British Columbia, dragon boat racing began over two thousand years ago on rivers in southern China. On the summer solstice, dragon boats were used to awaken and encourage the water deity, a dragon, to provide the rains necessary for abundant crops. The dragon was considered a good and heavenly creature, and human and other sacrifices were made to please it. Dragon boats were originally made by hollowing out great trees, and they could exceed one hundred feet in length and hold up to eighty people. With time, they became shorter and were designed to look more like dragons, with fierce heads, elaborate tails, and colourful scales. Chinese dragon boat festivals became the second most popular events of the year, after the New Year's festival, and hosting them was thought to bring health, happiness, and prosperity to the community.

Modern organized dragon boat racing began with the international competitions first held in Hong Kong in 1976. The boats used in this era were made from the strong and durable teak wood found in Thailand and Burma. They were only thirty-nine feet in length and were referred to by the Chinese as "canoes" to distinguish them from the "dragon boats" that were typically over fifty feet in length. The shorter length was inspired, in part, by the desire to be able to ship the boats in forty-foot containers.

Dragon boats made their North American debut in Vancouver in 1986. In fact, this was the first time they were seen anywhere outside of Asia. The Chinese Cultural Centre of Vancouver was looking for a way to commemorate Vancouver's one hundredth anniversary and contribute to Expo '86, whose theme was world transportation and communication. Organizers settled on the idea of introducing the traditional Chinese summer solstice festival, complete with dragon boats, to the exposition and brought over six teak boats from Hong Kong. Working with an organizer of the Hong Kong races, the centre ran instruction and training sessions in False Creek for the newly formed teams of people who generally had no background in the sport. The boats were then used in Canada's first-ever dragon boat races that summer as well as for ceremonial purposes celebrating traditional Chinese culture.

One of the racers that summer was Hugh Fisher, the Olympic gold medalist in sprint canoe-kayaking. He had seen a poster advertising dragon boating, thought it looked fantastic, and put together a crew that included some paddlers who were experienced in other disciplines. His team won the race at Expo and a free trip to the international races in Hong Kong, where they earned a silver medal, the first team from outside Asia ever to stand on the podium. A group of women introduced to the sport at Expo '86 went on to form the False Creek Women's Dragon Boat team. They took second place in the women's races in Hong Kong in 1988 and first place in 1989 and in four of the five subsequent years that they entered those races. British Columbian dragon boat racers were quickly making their mark internationally.

There were a number of reasons the women did so well and became the unofficial world champions in dragon boating for many years. Don Irvine was their coach and brought with him all the paddling skills and knowledge he had acquired as a sprint canoe-kayak competitor in the 1984 Olympics. The women, who were already strong competitors on the Vancouver dragon boating circuit, were attracted to the team from other clubs because of the organization's desire to race and win internationally. They trained three times a week on the water from December to May, sometimes having to break ice during the winter months. The final team selection was based on individual time trials. They were dedicated, organized, and focused.

Another reason for the team's victories was their manager, Vincent Lo, who emigrated from Hong Kong to Vancouver in 1974. Lo worked on the dragon boat festival at Expo '86 and took up the sport the following year, falling in love with the camaraderie and the beautiful practice environment before being asked to manage the region's top men's and women's teams. The only problem was that the teams had very limited access to dragon boats. The owners of the six teak boats that were featured at Expo were reluctant to allow them to be used for non-festival or non-ceremonial purposes because they didn't want to run the risk of the boats' hulls cracking in cold temperatures. Instead, the teams had to practise in ten-person voyageur canoes while their competitors in Asia trained in real dragon boats.

Lo decided to tackle the problem head on and build two dragon boats for the teams to use. After all, he had built a sixteen-foot cedar strip canoe and reasoned that the dragon boat was just a bigger canoe. He was also determined to design a dragon boat better suited for BC conditions. His boats were forty-eight feet long and made to accommodate twenty-four paddlers, rather than the standard thirty-nine-foot length for twenty paddlers. Although races used only twenty paddlers, extras were required on the team to accommodate last-minute injuries and illnesses, and the greater capacity allowed the entire team to practise at once without having to return to shore regularly to rotate paddlers. Lo's boats were also a foot wider than the standard dragon boat, and they had more space between seats, accommodating larger North American bodies and making the boats essentially untippable. He built them from fibreglass, with BC cedar inside the hull, making them more durable, light, and cold resistant. He argued they were closer in size to the original Chinese dragon boats. Manufactured in Hong

Kong, these were the first fibreglass dragon boats in the world to measure in at longer than forty feet.

Hong Kong–born Dr. David C. Lam was appointed BC's Lieutenant-Governor in September 1988 and believed his job was to be a "healer of wounds, a matchmaker of sorts between people of different views."[8] He noticed a rise in social and racial tensions in Vancouver at the time coinciding with an influx of immigrants from Asia and elsewhere, and he believed a dragon boat festival would promote racial harmony and cross-cultural understanding. He teamed up with prominent businessman Milton K. Wong to found the Canadian International Dragon Boat Festival Society, which has hosted dragon boat races in False Creek every summer since 1989. Although dragon boat festivals are now held in every province of Canada, this is the longest-running one outside of Asia and still one of the biggest and best in North America.

The False Creek festival retains some of the key traditions from its Chinese heritage, including being held near the summer solstice, honouring the dragon as a kind creature, using boats shaped and decorated to resemble dragons, and having Taoist priests perform the "awakening of the dragons" blessing ceremony followed by the application of red paint to the dragon's eyes to give it sight. Breaking from tradition, participants do not pray for rain (it's plentiful enough in Vancouver!), and no humans are sacrificed! And, unlike many other North American dragon boat festivals, this one focuses on celebrating cultural diversity through culinary, visual, and performing arts in addition to the races themselves. The Lieutenant-Governor's paddle is passed among festival participants as they celebrate the "spirit of the dragon"—the coming together and working as a team for a common goal.

As the sport of dragon boating continued to grow around the world, the International Dragon Boat Federation (IDBF) was formed in 1991. While some believed the sport should be included in the International Canoe Federation (ICF), the important cultural, ceremonial, and religious dimensions of dragon boating were key factors in the creation of this new international body. The IDBF held their first world championships in China in 1995, and the second championships were held a year later in Vancouver in recognition of that city's role in introducing dragon boating outside of Asia ten years earlier.

Vincent Lo's dragon boats gained increasing public recognition. The first two were very popular in Vancouver, and the Canadian International Dragon Boat Festival Society wanted a fleet for their annual races. Faced with prohibitive transportation costs for craft longer than could be enclosed in the standard shipping containers, Lo and his partner Don Irvine began building them locally. Before long, their Six-Sixteen boats, named after the series of strokes commonly used at the start of dragon boat races, with their distinctive maple leaf symbol and beautiful dragon heads and tails, were seen everywhere in False Creek. Their popularity spread up and down the west coast and even to the east coast, despite the high transportation costs. Demand slowed when the IDBF made the thirty-nine-foot models the standard for their races, but Lo, now the sole owner, has built over two hundred boats to date and continues to build several a year on a part-time basis.

The growing popularity of dragon boating inspired an unlikely development in the field of medicine. In 1995, Dr. Don McKenzie, a sports medicine physician working at UBC, wanted to test his theory that upper body exercise could be beneficial for breast cancer patients. The conventional thinking at that time was that such exercise could increase the risk of lymphedema, the painful, irreversible swelling of the arm and chest area that sometimes occurred after surgery and radiation treatment. With McKenzie's background as a coach and physician for the Canadian canoe-kayak team at five Olympics Games, dragon boating seemed like the perfect test, and he recruited twenty-four women to participate in a carefully controlled experiment in a boat on False Creek in 1996.

Jane Frost was one of those women. She had been first diagnosed with breast cancer in 1986 when she was only thirty-six years of age. Following treatment, she had been told to avoid upper body exercise, which included everything from golf and tennis to gardening, knitting, and even playing the piano, for the rest of her life. It was a very restrictive program, and being free of it would be life changing. Although they were wary of the possible side effects and some were discouraged from participating by their friends and family, the women who volunteered for McKenzie's dragon boating experiment wanted that freedom. They bravely decided to proceed and called their craft *Abreast in a Boat*. McKenzie's theory was proved correct: not one of the team members developed lymphedema as a result of the paddling, and the accepted protocol following breast cancer treatment began to change across the medical profession.

But the story didn't end there. The women considered their boat a floating support group and developed fast friendships. They decided to celebrate the conclusion of the testing by entering the Vancouver Dragon Boat Festival wearing their distinctive pink outfits. They welcomed the associated publicity because they wanted all those living with breast cancer to be able to live full and active lives. In the following year's Vancouver festival, three local teams of breast cancer patients were among the participants. The original team then set their sights on the 1998 Wellington Dragon Boat Festival in New Zealand. Despite tipping twice in practice using smaller boats in rough conditions, they persevered and finished third in a race against teams who did not face the same health challenges as they did. But more importantly, they spread the word about dragon boating after breast cancer and helped break the silence about the disease in countries around the world.

As the movement spread, Jane Frost spearheaded the creation of the International Breast Cancer Paddlers' Commission (IBCPC), becoming its founding and current president. The group's first dragon boat festival, 10 Years Abreast, was held in Vancouver in 2005 and attracted more than eighteen hundred breast cancer survivors. There are now over one hundred member teams from a dozen countries, with Canada having the strongest representation, including twelve teams from BC. Boat names reflecting the underlying spirit of the cause include *Bosom Buddies*, *Breast Friends*, *Breast Strokes*, *Busting with Energy*, *Busting with Life*, *CanSurvive*, *Chestmates*, *Dragon Divas*, *Healing Dragons*, *Hope Afloat*, *Simply the Breast*, *Spirit Warriors*, *Survivor Thrivers*, and *Wonder Broads*. In addition to encouraging those who have been diagnosed with breast cancer, the movement also seeks to raise awareness about the disease and the importance of regular exercise, healthy nutrition, and not smoking.

Dr. McKenzie continued his involvement after the conclusion of the experiment, coaching the original team for many years. Reflecting on the impact of the program, he commented:

> It has been a marvelous experience . . . I have been able to see what Abreast in a Boat *has done for so many women— the effect has been so profound on their emotions and so positive globally. The people I've met, the camaraderie, the support they get from other cancer patients, that has been the miracle of the whole project. The lymphedema was the start. Now it's a small part of it.*[9]

At the time of writing, all but one of the original twenty-four team members of *Abreast in a Boat* are still alive, and at least one of them describes dragon boating as "the best thing I ever did."

I was particularly interested in the journey of the breast cancer paddlers since I had been diagnosed with prostate cancer in 2005. I too found support by talking to others with the same diagnosis, and through them I heard about BC-based InspireHealth, Canada's foremost integrative cancer care centre. Working with their medical professionals, I learned about the importance of good nutrition, exercise, and emotional support in aiding recovery after treatment and reducing the risks of recurrence. I subsequently made significant changes in my lifestyle.

The concept of using dragon boating as a way for people with a medical condition to get both exercise and support has spread far beyond breast cancer and is now well established in BC. A team of paddlers with kidney failure, for example, practices on False Creek every month but January. They formed in 2001 to promote physical health and emotional well-being, and to raise public awareness about organ donation. They are coached by a volunteer with twenty-five years of dragon boating experience and always have medical professionals on board. Their renal systems are often in poor shape and they typically need four hours of dialysis, three times a week. Nevertheless, they travel to compete and are proud of the gold medal they won against healthy paddlers in San Francisco. If their numbers get too low to race in the latter part of the season, they sometimes merge with members of the team with multiple sclerosis.

Paddlers united by various medical conditions have found creative and humorous names for their boats that reflect their optimism and hope. Some of the participating boats, and their associated conditions, include:

- *Conquering Waves* (mental impairment)
- *Eye of the Dragon* (visual impairment)
- *Gift of Life* (transplant recipients)

- *Grandragons* (aging)
- *Off Balance* (multiple sclerosis)
- *Off 2 P* (kidney failure)

Dragon boating appeals to a wide range of people and is one of the fastest growing team sports in Canada. The False Creek Racing Canoe Club has become the largest paddling club in Canada. Like many of the other paddling clubs in BC, it offers a range of craft, but dragon boating occupies a special place. Because it is a relatively easy sport to learn and does not require any particular strengths or skills, it serves as an excellent introduction to paddling. Some paddlers later switch over to smaller canoes, either for additional race preparation or recreational use.

Dragon boating also has other characteristics that help account for its growth. It's a very inclusive sport, appealing to young and old, men and women, and a variety of cultures. While perhaps initially seen as a Chinese sport, it has become very mainstream in North America. As all the paddlers have identical roles and must work to support each other, companies sometimes use the sport as a team-building exercise with benefits reaching back into the workplace. It also has a strong social component, keeping teams together throughout and beyond the season. Once paddlers find a boat culture they like, matching their desired degree of competitiveness, they can stick with it for years.

———

Another one of the fastest-growing sports in BC is outrigger canoeing—and I wanted to try it. On an August morning in 2012, I joined a group of seniors from the False Creek Racing Canoe Club on one of their regular practices on English Bay. Many had just returned from the World Outrigger Sprint Championships in Calgary, where Canada had finished third overall; some of the members had won gold, silver, and bronze medals in individual events. The group of about twenty practises two mornings a week year-round (except when the temperature falls below zero), and goes to Hawaii for two weeks in January to paddle at their sister club.

I paddled in a six-person forty-four-foot fibreglass canoe with an attached float, known as an ama, on the left side. We headed out in heavy rain, which later ended, on a calm but rolling sea. I followed the moderately fast pace set by the lead paddlers and switched sides every twelfth stroke at the call of the third paddler. I was reminded of my dragon boating experience, with the similar commands of "paddles up," "take it away," and, best of all, "let 'er run." I also appreciated the longer stroke, the greater space between paddles, the ability to switch sides, and the back support provided. Although the regulars all had stories of tipping in an outrigger canoe (the group was called the HULIgans, derived from *huli*, meaning "tip" in Hawaiian), I found the craft very stable. We were on the water for two hours, with short breaks about every thirty minutes.

Outrigger canoes date back several thousand years in the Indian and Pacific Oceans, where they were used to travel between islands. Strong outrigger canoe cultures developed in areas of Polynesia, but faded with the growing influence of Europeans. In the last century, there was a revival of this culture with outrigger canoe races in Tahiti, Hawaii, and New Zealand. In Canada, the interest in these canoes started in BC in the 1980s and grew rapidly in the 1990s. The initial demand here arose in part from the desire by dragon boaters to practise in smaller craft between outings with their full team. Soon it caught on as a sport in its own right.

An early Canadian entrant to this market was the Canadian Class Racer, a six-person outrigger canoe (OC-6) designed and produced by Calmar Paints and Fibreglass Ltd. in North Vancouver.

They produced a variety of fibreglass products and tried their hand at canoes before superior designs pushed them out of that market. Roy Vickers observed the fibreglass outrigger canoes in Hawaii and went to Western Canoeing and Kayaking in Abbotsford to see if they could build a modern version of the traditional Haida ocean-going canoe. This led to the creation of the Northern Dancer fibreglass canoes designed by James van Nostrand that were used in the 1997 VisionQuest journey. Western then wondered if they could use their capability of building big canoes to build an OC-6. Van Nostrand worked with US canoeist Greg Barton to design the forty-five foot Advantage, which was introduced to the market in 1998. They have also produced a four-person outrigger canoe, which they are planning to reintroduce.

After his involvement with VisionQuest, Ed Hill wondered how to introduce canoeing more actively in his community. The result was the first Howe Sound Outrigger Canoe Race in 1999, based out of Gibsons, which continues to this day. Melanie Whittall, a former BC sea kayak instructor who was working at a paddlesport retail store, saw the difficulty in acquiring enough small outrigger canoes to meet local demand and bought the mould for the US-designed OC-1 Sea Lion. Working with van Nostrand and Western Canoeing and Kayaking, she created the C Lion OC-1 and entered it in one of the early Howe Sound Races. Both the Advantage and C Lion have proved popular and are still on the market. The Howe Sound races have become Canada's signature long-distance outrigger canoe races, hosting Canada's national championships and attracting paddlers from around the world. Outrigger canoe racing in Canada continues to be a predominantly BC-centred sport, and competitions are held most weekends throughout the province from April until October.

Just as dragon boating retains some of its original Asian cultural elements, outrigger canoeing has kept many of its Polynesian influences. The canoe was very important to Polynesians historically, given its role in populating the islands, and a strong canoe culture remains. In Hawaii, canoeing is more than a sport and is part of the "Aloha spirit" of cherishing and protecting the earth, sky, and sea. The Polynesian impact is apparent in BC in the naming of rigging, the blessing of races, and the culinary and other rituals at outrigger events. One tradition that hasn't transferred well here is the "water change" in longer races. This involves dropping some rested crew members in the path of their canoe and having them replace their tired colleagues by clambering into their vacated spots as the boat passes. The tired paddlers are later retrieved from the water by a support boat, allowed to replenish their energy, and eventually return to their canoe in the same wet way. The colder waters of BC reduce the attractiveness of this method, so a "shore change" at a convenient beach is more popular here.

———

My wife and I love to visit the small town of Pemberton, located in a fertile valley surrounded by spectacular mountains and less than a half-hour's drive north of Whistler. Every summer we camp at a provincial park just south of town. One year, we decided to visit the nearby One Mile Lake Park. This area has been home to the Lil'wat people for centuries, as evidenced by ancient pictographs and petroglyphs, along with trees whose bark had been partially removed for the many traditional uses of cedar. Coho salmon spawn in the creek feeding the lake before beginning their long journey to the Fraser River and the Pacific Ocean. Magnificent old cedar and Douglas fir trees populate the far side of the lake and provide shelter to the black bears and mule deer in the area. What particularly caught my eye at One Mile Lake, though, was a "boat house" near the water that contained more than fifty canoes of various shapes and sizes, including voyageur canoes, dragon boats, and large outrigger canoes. I was amazed a body of water that was at least a quarter full of water lilies and, at most, a kilometre in circumference was home to such a fleet. After doing a little digging and talking to Dr. Hugh Fisher and others, I learned the true story of canoeing on what locals affectionately refer to as "One Mile Puddle."

Prior to his gold medal win at the 1984 Olympics, Hugh Fisher spent his winters training in California. There, he started to practise in outrigger canoes and joined a team that won the biggest outrigger canoe race in the world, the Molokai Hoe, which traversed the more than sixty-four kilometres of open ocean between two Hawaiian islands. After winning at the Olympics, he went to medical school at UBC and started the False Creek Racing Canoe Club, where he became very active in dragon boating. He went to New Zealand to do his internship and put together a dragon boat team that went on to win the New Zealand Championships. He then moved to Pemberton, where he practised as a family doctor. One patient said she had heard about his racing background and asked him if he would teach her daughter how to row. He explained that he had a paddling, not a rowing, background and would be happy to teach her that.

Thus began a canoeing program on tiny One Mile Lake. Before long, students from the Pemberton Secondary School and the neighbouring Mount Currie First Nations Community School combined to field a team called the Laoyam Eagles, reflecting the mascot names of both schools. At first they used aluminum voyageur canoes, but later they acquired two dragon boats. The lake could only offer a straight run of 250 metres, so the crews became skilled at turning in training for races of up to 2,000 metres. The teams became so good at doing short, fast banked turns that race rules were changed to require wider turns. In 1999, they entered the False Creek Dragon Boat Festival and won the junior A category, beginning an unbroken streak of victories there that has continued to this day. The Pemberton–area teams have gone on to win the Junior Titles at both the Canadian national championships and the World Dragon Boat Racing Championships and have contributed heavily to successful Canadian national teams. Recently, an outrigger canoeing program started on the lake, and a paddler named Aleea Dahinden became the first Canadian junior girl to ever win an outrigger world championship medal. The students have also taken home dozens of medals in other canoeing disciplines at the BC Games. Rival teams have been curious about how they do it and have been amazed when they see the size of the lake the students train on.

So how *do* they do it? How do Pemberton and Mount Currie, with a combined population of less than five thousand and a little lake that remains frozen until April, turn out world champion teams? Everyone attributes the success to Hugh Fisher, who continues to race and won individual and team gold medals at the 2012 World Outrigger Championships. At this point, his whole family is involved; his wife is the president of the Pemberton Canoe and Kayak Club and his daughter runs a summer paddling program for younger children. The whole Pemberton–area community is engaged, too, with adults winning medals at dragon boating and outrigger championships. One woman was crowned world champion at an outrigger event.

The program has had a big impact on some of those involved. Tachona Jones, an Aboriginal teenager and UBC student who has travelled as far as Hungary to compete in dragon boating events after her start on One Mile Lake, says the experience changed her life. She says she now believes she is capable of doing well if she applies herself and doesn't think she would be where she is if she hadn't done dragon boating. "It inspired lots of kids and made a lot of people in Pemberton proud," she said in a conversation with me. "Hugh Fisher and [team manager] Karen Tomlinson helped make our dreams come true."[10]

The paddlers I talked to describe Fisher as a wonderful coach, able to really motivate people with his low-key style. "The best coach in the world" is how one teen paddler put it. Fisher himself says that while he does teach paddling technique and seeks to develop strength and endurance, his priority is to get children on the water and encourage them to have fun. He believes that every grade six student in Canada should learn how to paddle a canoe and hopes he is introducing young people to a lifelong pastime. This Order of Canada holder's influence is felt well beyond Pemberton. Other BC paddling leaders speak of how he helped them and helped advance the sport of canoeing in the province. Indeed, Ontario-based Larry Cain, another Canadian Olympic canoeing gold medalist, says Fisher has been very influential in various canoeing disciplines across the country.

———

British Columbia is a leader in various disciplines of canoe racing, including dragon boats and outriggers, as well as less serious canoe and kayak competitions. UBC's annual Day of the Longboat, with over three thousand participants, claims to be "the largest voyageur canoe race in the world." Costumed paddlers start from a beach, jump into their canoes, paddle along a course, land at another beach to pick up a mallet, return to the starting beach, and use the mallet to ring a large bell on shore. Many participants have never been in a canoe until the practice the week before the event.

For smaller craft, "North America's largest weekly paddlesport race" runs out of Deep Cove every summer. The event attracts kayakers, canoeists, stand-up paddleboarders (where the paddler stands on a surfboard-like craft propelled with a long paddle), and other paddlers. The fleet can exceed one hundred boats and follows a course that changes from week to week. One race, usually held on a warmer day, involves two-boat teams. The team starts together, then one boat heads to an island and the other to the mainland. After landing, the teammates run and swim to the other boat, passing en route, then paddle their teammate's boat back to a rendezvous point and finish together. The races are video-taped and paddlers later go to the local pub to watch the results over beer. Some of the people in these races take them quite seriously, and an increasing number race in a fast surf ski—a long, narrow, lightweight craft that the racer sits on top of in an open cockpit. The dominant local brand of surf ski is the "think" kayak, which is owned by a Deep Cove resident and regular participant in the races. It is now sold worldwide and is doing well on the international racing circuit. At one race I attended, three participants were headed to the World Surfski Championships in Portugal the following week, and several of the younger paddlers were preparing to go to the Canada Summer Games in Quebec.

Hugh Fisher clearly had a significant impact on different types of canoe development and racing in British Columbia and beyond. After winning an Olympic gold medal, he co-founded what has become the largest racing canoe club in Canada and started another club in a very small community that has consistently produced national and world champion paddlers. Others from Canadian Olympic canoe-kayaking teams have also gone on to paddle and coach dragon boats and outrigger canoes. Indeed, competitive paddlers often practise and race in several types of canoes. Following the trade of a solo dugout canoe for a solo outrigger canoe, the latter has become popular with some Salish racers, particularly in their off-season.

The different types of racing canoes share other similarities beyond paddling crews. The designs and materials evolved in the quest to achieve greater speed, often with BC creators and builders at the forefront of these changes. The traditional spiritual dimensions were often maintained, whether in the figurehead of the dragon or sea wolf, or in the rituals surrounding the preparation for and participation in races. They all involved a considerable amount of personal and team development, from the basics of learning strokes and staying dry to the more advanced skills of working together and mastering the different stages of a race. Some went even further, helping to heal relationships between different cultures or heal people with medical challenges by providing them with a floating emotional support group.

chapter six ——

SYMBOLIC CANOES

WHEN I was a child, I had a coin collection. My favourite piece was the Canadian silver dollar, which featured an idyllic scene of a birchbark canoe on the back. The canoe took up the full width the coin, with a fur trader in the stern and a First Nations person in the bow, paddling their cargo-laden craft past an island with two wind-swept pine trees bathed in the northern lights. That coin introduced me to the power of the canoe as a symbol.

Over the years, the silver dollar got smaller, nickel replaced the silver, and finally its production ceased in 1986. When the Royal Canadian Mint announced plans to introduce a new, smaller, bronze-plated coin in 1987 to replace the dollar bill, the same canoe image was supposed to appear on the back. However, the master die for the new piece was lost in shipment from Ottawa to Winnipeg, and the Mint decided to craft a new design to eliminate the risk of counterfeiting. That is how the loon replaced the canoe on what is now known as the loonie. It is interesting to speculate what the coin, and our national currency, would be known as had this substitution not occurred.

Despite the disappearance of the silver dollar and its "symbolic canoe," the canoe continues to have symbolic significance. John Jennings wrote in 1999, "The canoe is a symbol unique to Canada. It is one of the greatest gifts of the First Peoples to all those who came after. It is the most powerful symbol joining the Native peoples to the two founding cultures of Europe—French and English. It is a symbol of exploration and discovery, of individual courage and of partnership, of heroic enterprise and of quiet harmony with Nature."[1] Jennings was speaking from a national and historical perspective. I was interested in discovering any symbolic value the canoe has in British Columbia today—a meaning that goes beyond transportation.

Of course, we have already seen some modern symbolic use of the canoe in this province. The "dancing canoes" in the Vancouver Olympics were part of a humorous Closing Ceremony that included giant Mounties, hockey players, beavers, and other iconic Canadian symbols. More seriously, we have seen how the canoe is at the heart of a resurgence in cultural identity and pride by the First Nations people in BC. But is there more?

In addition to marking the end of the silver dollar, the year 1986 saw the beginning of a new canoe-based symbol that would become important for Canada. After successfully designing and building his fifty-foot ocean-going canoe *Lootaas* for Expo '86 in Vancouver, Bill Reid turned his attention to creating a sculpture for the Canadian Embassy in Washington, DC. Five years later, *The Spirit of Haida Gwaii: The Black Canoe* was completed and installed in the US capital. The black-coated bronze casting depicts thirteen passengers in a twenty-foot Haida-style ocean-going canoe. The occupants are important Haida icons—the raven and eagle, as well as bears, a beaver, a fish, a mouse, a wolf, and a frog, along with several people. On closer inspection, however, the species are blurred as some of the figures have mixed human and animal characteristics, consistent with the Haida belief in the transformation of living creatures and the interconnection of all life. Although there is some fighting and biting among the passengers, it's clear they're on a journey together. What's not as clear is their purpose and direction and whether the chief, standing in the centre, or the Raven, steering at the back, is in charge. The Canadian government's purchase of the sculpture and its placement in Washington suggested to one BC observer "that the canoe, with all it implies, has been adopted as the official symbol of the country."[2]

Bolstering this view is the prominent placement of other replicas of *The Spirit of Haida Gwaii*. A full-sized white plaster version of the work rests in the Canadian Museum of History in Gatineau, Quebec. The sculpture is at one end of the Grand Hall, with its towering BC totem poles and Aboriginal house facades, and is the site of many government receptions. UBC-educated First Nations architect Douglas Cardinal was inspired by the myth of Raven's magic canoe to design the hall in the shape of an enormous canoe. According to the legend, Raven's canoe could shrink to the size of a pine needle, and this is illustrated in the ceiling of the Grand Hall, which has smaller canoe shapes embedded within larger ones. And so, Bill Reid's magnificent black and white canoe sculptures reside in the capitals of the two countries whose cultures and common boundaries have been most influenced by the canoe and to remind visitors that we are all—people and animals—on a journey together.

A third full-sized copy of this sculpture, known commonly as the *Jade Canoe*, is the focal point of the Vancouver International Airport (YVR). It sits in the centre of a semicircular amphitheatre where travellers can relax while waiting for flights. The green finish has been touched by so many hands that the underlying bronze casting shows in multiple places. This, along with a collection of other full-sized BC-built canoes and kayaks in the terminal, suggests the canoe is an important symbol at what is arguably BC's modern crossroads.

A fourth version of Bill Reid's masterpiece revived the symbol of the canoe on Canadian currency for the first time since the silver dollar was discontinued. From 2004 to 2011, the *Black Canoe* appeared on the back of the Canadian twenty-dollar bill. The symbolism had evolved from a fairly stereotypical image of a voyageur canoe in the Canadian wilderness to a more complex one showing a different side of First Nations culture, exploring our relationship with nature and our complex cultural identity.

Another work with a similar message is the dugout canoe that then-Lieutenant-Governor Steven Point carved in 2009 and which is now on display at the BC legislative building. Mr. Point, a former chief of the Skowkale Nation and a strong supporter of the revived big canoe journeys, found a partially carved ten-foot river canoe near his official residence in Victoria and worked to complete it at a Government House garage during his spare time. Calling it the "unity" canoe project, he said: "I look at the world as one canoe, and we're all paddling in it together."[3] Upon completion of his term in office, he elaborated: "The canoe project was about reconciliation and how do we get people to better understand each other and begin talking and to break down barriers . . . We really have to turn the page on history and begin to think a lot about how we're going to work together in the future"[4]

BC canoes figure prominently in many other works of public art across the province. One with quite a different message is Ken Lum's *Four Boats Stranded: Red and Yellow, Black and White*, a large work that sits on the roof of the Vancouver Art Gallery. The work can be viewed as a comment on immigration and acculturation and features four model boats: a First Nations ocean-going canoe, a cargo ship,[5] the steamliner *Komagata Maru*,[6] and George Vancouver's ship HMS *Discovery*. Each vessel has been placed at one of the building's compass points and is painted in a colour to reflect the stereotyped racial vision presented in the hymn "Jesus Loves the Little Children." The canoe is red and rests on the north corner. To me, the four vessels stranded on the four corners of the building suggest racial discrimination or a lack of unity, despite attempts to use Christianity as a common religion. The work is a reminder of a painful and divided past whose legacy still persists.

Aboriginal artists have used the canoe to communicate a variety of perspectives. In many cases, the art highlights the significance of the canoe to Native traditions and culture and is a way to express people's identity. In some cases, though, it is used to tell a difficult story. For example, Jason Nahanee, a Squamish Nation member who attended the St. Paul's Indian Residential School in North Vancouver, is designing and carving a monument dedicated to the more than two thousand First Nations children who were forced to live at the school from 1898 to 1959. The monument's plaque will show an ocean-going dugout canoe being paddled from the trough of a wave, representing the era of the residential schools and the loss of Native culture through to the wave's crest and the revival of traditions. "The wave going up on the other side represents our people gaining their language rights back and their culture,"[7] said another former St. Paul's student.

———

The canoe has also been used symbolically at many important events. We saw earlier how various canoes were used in BC to transport the Olympic flame en route to opening the 2010 Winter Games in Vancouver and how voyageur canoes "danced" across the stage in the Games' Closing Ceremony. The Opening Ceremony also featured a canoe—a bright blue flying voyageur canoe with a horned fiddler in it. It was inspired by "La Chasse-galerie," a popular French-Canadian tale of voyageurs in the woods who made a deal with the devil to enable them to visit their sweethearts in a flying canoe.

Another ceremonial event featuring a Canadian canoe was the Thames Diamond Jubilee Pageant in honour of Queen Elizabeth II's sixty years on the throne, on June 3, 2012. The Canadian government wanted to have a canoe represent the country in this event and worked with James Raffan at the Canadian Canoe Museum to find a suitable candidate. They initially nominated a thirty-six-foot voyageur canoe made from birchbark for the occasion, but the British authorities deemed it unseaworthy. The government then agreed that Bill Reid's Haida Gwaii–based *Lootaas*, to be manned by fourteen Haida paddlers, would be the ideal representative. But less than two months before the pageant, *Lootaas* reportedly developed a large crack and had to withdraw.

A search began in earnest to find an appropriate replacement. A twenty-six-foot fibreglass voyageur *Canot du nord*, or North canoe, that had last been used in the 2008 Thompson Brigade was found. The thirty-year-old canoe was being stored in a field, with accompanying mould, small holes, and resident animals, but it was turned into a craft "fit for a Queen" in less than two weeks. Raffan flew with the canoe in an otherwise empty 174-foot-long RCAF C-17 transport from Trenton, Ontario, to England in time for the crew of eight Canadians to have one quick practice on the Thames before the big event.

Canada One/Un, as the Canadian vessel was named, was painted to look like birchbark and was paddled by a crew dressed in voyageur-period attire seated behind a large Canadian flag. Despite headwinds, rain, and four-foot waves, the canoe was able to maintain the four-knot pace of the flotilla comprising over a thousand boats along the twenty-two-kilometre course. From the stern of the canoe, Raffan even managed a live interview with CBC's Peter Mansbridge, although the resulting lapse in steering duties nearly caused a collision. And because of the last-minute substitution, official documents still showed that Canada was represented by a Haida canoe. It is interesting to think about the different messages the three candidate canoes convey.

The other boat in the flotilla sporting a large Canadian flag was the dragon boat *Abreast from the West* with an all–British Columbia crew of women who had been diagnosed with breast cancer. The women had practised together in their own boat on the Fraser River, but for the pageant they borrowed a British boat, appropriately painted red and white. Vancouver's Jane Frost, who started the International Breast Cancer Paddlers' Commission, was in another dragon boat with a crew of breast cancer survivors from eight countries. The boat was steered by Don McKenzie, the BC doctor who began what has become a global movement to keep women active after their cancer treatment.

Another important event in which canoes played a critical symbolic role occurred in Vancouver in September 2013 when the Truth and Reconciliation Commission of Canada (TRC) came to hear from survivors of Aboriginal residential schools. Although the Commission had visited many other parts of Canada, this was the first event of its kind to be welcomed by a canoe gathering. While waiting for the ceremonies to begin, I talked with the woman beside me who was visiting from the Nass Valley, north of Prince Rupert. I told her of my visit to her area ten years before and my sighting of the elusive kermode bear there. She told me about her childhood and how she had been taken in a school bus from her home on the coast to a residential school in Edmonton, over a thousand kilometres away, returning home only for summer breaks. She said the school had become a "dry out" centre after its closure, which I thought somewhat ironic, before it burnt down.

After the host First Nations had welcomed everyone, the canoes began to arrive. The first flotilla contained leaders from the different nations, including Shawn Atleo, national chief of the Assembly of First Nations. Next came groups of canoes with people from different areas of the province and beyond, followed by a cluster of non-Aboriginal paddlers. Some participants wore traditional Native clothing and cedar hats while others wore more contemporary "Journey of Reconciliation" T-shirts. Speakers in the canoes sought permission to come ashore and brought messages for the large audience assembled at False Creek.

The speakers in the canoes and on the receiving platform spoke of the physical, emotional, and cultural impact of the residential school policy on the children who attended, their parents, and subsequent generations, and of the need to speak the truth about this in order to help the healing process. Some spoke deliberately to non-Native people, saying other Canadians must feel the shame of this experience, open their hearts and minds, and listen to what the First Nations people have to offer. The recurring theme was the need to move forward in a closer relationship within Canada in the spirit of reconciliation. "Today marks a new beginning and the start of a massive resurgence of our culture," declared Chief Atleo. The ceremonies concluded with the handing of a talking stick to Justice Murray Sinclair, the head of the Commission.

The day had a big impact on me. I was moved when my neighbour cried as she heard the speaker in the canoe from her home in the Nass Valley. I was also moved by the use of canoes in the ceremony, the explicit reference to them as symbols of healing, and the recognition that we are all ultimately in the same boat. I was thrilled to see sixty canoes of varying types and sizes—ocean-going, racing, dragon, voyageur, and kayak—all paddling together and parading by BC Place. And I was struck by the diversity of non-Native groups represented, including police and other government organizations, churches, communities, and corporations. When the paddlers were all thumping their upright paddles in unison to a drumming song, it was possible to feel Reconciliation Canada's message of "*Namwayut*—we are all one."

There was that canoe-related theme again—that we are all one. We saw it in *The Spirit of Haida Gwaii* and Steven Point's unity canoe project. In fact, it's been a recurring message in the Canoe Brigades honouring all races and the river, in the Pulling Together journeys linking authority figures and Native youth, and in the dragon boat races introducing Asian traditions to non-Asian paddlers. It was seen with Fisher and Morris working together to win an Olympic gold medal and during the Day of the Longboat uniting a university community.

———

Another aspect of the emerging symbolism of the canoe in BC is that of unity with nature. For example, the Rivershed Society of British Columbia runs an annual Sustainable Living Leadership Program in which young adults paddle down most of the Fraser River, from headwaters to the ocean, in voyageur canoes and inflatable rafts. Inspired by MP Fin Donnelly's swims of the length of the Fraser to raise awareness for environmental impacts on rivers, the program is a twenty-five-day floating classroom where participants experience the people and environment along one of the world's greatest salmon runs. Along the way they learn about the area's past and present, gain a deeper understanding of sustainability, and develop a commitment to preserving the natural environment in their own communities. Although this trip could be done in a powerboat, it is hard to image that it would have the same effect on participants.

Another canoe-based educational trip was the Great Bear Rainforest Youth Paddle in June 2012. Organized by students from Quest University Canada in Squamish who teamed up with First Nations high school students from the mid-coast community of Hartley Bay, the four-day paddling trip traversed some of the channels where supertankers are proposed to carry oil from Kitimat en route to the US and China. The students saw killer and humpback whales and sea lions from their large, fibreglass, eighteen-person, ocean-going canoe. They learned about the huge ecotourism potential of the area, and about the expected impact on marine life from the noise of supertankers and potential oil spills. "Youth from two culturally different backgrounds have banded together along a proposed route that could be devastated in one twist, one slip of a wheel,"[8] said Cam Hill, a Hartley Bay high school teacher and band-elected council member. The canoe appeared to be the ideal craft to forge a sense of unity among the paddlers and between the students and their environment.

The use of BC canoes to reinforce the unity theme has not been limited to young people; they are being employed in ecotourism aimed at broader markets as well. The most ambitious use of a west coast canoe for the tourist market was done by Seashore Charters, owned by the Metlakatla Development Corporation in Prince Rupert. This group wanted to use the longest northwest coast dugout-style canoe in existence, which meant it had to outdo the 1904 sixty-three-foot northern style canoe at the American Museum of Natural History in New York. They approached canoe designer James van Nostrand, who created the Dancer series of dugout-style canoes for Western Canoeing and Kayaking. His initial reaction was that a canoe that long would be too unwieldy and uncomfortable for tourists on day trips. But after researching further the large canoes still in existence or captured in photographs, and taking into account modern materials, he concluded that it could be done. And so it was that a sixty-five-foot fibreglass dugout-style canoe, complete with beautiful First Nations art and a regulation inflatable life raft, was delivered to Prince Rupert in the spring of 2010 to serve up to forty cruise-ship passengers. The canoe is so long, in fact, that it has its own internal public address system to keep passengers informed, and uses two-way radios to communicate instructions between the bow and stern paddlers.

The elders named the canoe *Ha'nda'wit'waada*, which means "Where people come together and get to know one another." The name appears most appropriate, given the mix of countries represented in the canoe over the course of a summer. The Metlakatla Development Corporation now boasts that they have "the largest north coastal First Nations canoe ever constructed," and "the largest canoe in North America."[9]

Another British Columbian to use the canoe as a unifying vehicle is Chris Cooper. Born in England and introduced to kayaking as a teenager after moving to the Vancouver area, Cooper went on to develop a professional guiding business and then built the largest fleet of historical voyageur canoes in Canada, which he used with corporate and school groups. Because of his experience with organizing long trips in big canoes, he helped train the RCMP members paddling on the 1997 VisionQuest journey and participated in that and many subsequent Pulling Together trips. From these adventures, he was inspired to use a canoe farther afield to help young people experience other cultures, learn about teamwork, and appreciate nature.

In 2004, Cooper sold his fleet of sixteen voyageur canoes to Dave Wooldridge, who expanded the business under the name Ridge Wilderness Adventures. Wooldridge continues to provide outings for educational purposes, primarily to young people through schools and various groups. Because BC is recognized as being the Canadian leader in big canoes, Paddle Canada, which oversees recreational paddling in the country, asked Wooldridge to develop an instructional program for users of these craft. That program is now the accepted standard, and Wooldridge, who is Canada's leading big-canoe instructor-trainer, has taught it in various canoeing countries around the world.

Cooper, meanwhile, focused his energies on *Spirit Dancer*. This forty-two-foot canoe, designed for the open ocean and built by Western Canoeing and Kayaking, combined features from various types of canoes used in this province. The craft began as a large, custom-built, fibreglass-and-wood, voyageur-style Montreal canoe made in BC with birchbark decor, a spray deck with fourteen sealable openings, adjustable outriggers with attached double kayaks, and two masts. Launched in 2004 with a traditional First Nations blessing, the new canoe went on a 2,000-kilometre, 105-day journey from Petersburg, Alaska, to Vancouver. It was now ready for Cooper's ultimate challenge.

Cooper's goal was to bring together youth from Canada and Britain to learn while circumnavigating the British Isles. Starting in London in May 2008, he paddled through the English Channel all along the south coast off Cornwall to the Isles of Scilly. He was then invited to the Orkney Islands off the north coast of Scotland and spent two summers there, followed by three summers even farther north in the Shetland Islands. He estimates that he paddled and sailed, using a large Canadian flag, more than 2,500 kilometres over those six summers.

Cooper told me that the reaction to his travels in the UK was extraordinary. Although this type of canoe was foreign to the areas he visited, the people, particularly those living on the smaller islands, had a strong interest in all things maritime and immersed themselves enthusiastically in this unique BC craft. For his part, Cooper was thrilled with the reception he received and the opportunity to introduce thousands of people to canoeing in such wild, beautiful, and remote areas. He gifted BC-made paddles to many of those who helped him en route and gave the canoe to the people of the Shetland Islands to help them fundraise for a youth exchange between the UK and British Columbia. There is now even talk of a possible trip in the canoe through the heart of Europe down the Danube River to the Black Sea.

Because of their knowledge and love of rivers, lakes, and oceans, some BC paddlers have been inspired to do more than just use canoes to educate others about the environment; some have been moved to try to protect and improve the health of waterways.

Mark Angelo, who has paddled every kilometre of the Fraser River, founded BC Rivers Day in 1980. This later grew to become World Rivers Day, which is now observed by millions of people in more than sixty countries. The annual event celebrates the value of rivers, educates people through canoe outings and others means, and acts to improve river health through garbage removal, habitat restoration, and stewardship initiatives. This small BC initiative turned global phenomenon reflects Anglo's belief that "Rivers are the arteries of our planet; they are lifelines in the truest sense."[10]

Canoes have also been used to focus attention on proposed BC developments that could harm rivers and oceans. During the 2012 racing canoe festival at Cates Park, Chief Justin George of the Tsleil-Waututh Nation spoke of his people's opposition to the Kinder Morgan proposal to more than double the capacity of the pipeline carrying oil to the terminal across from the park and the resulting increase in the number of tankers traversing local waters. Building on the signs containing the profile of an ocean-going canoe that welcomes people entering their reserve, and reinforcing the recurring unity theme, George said, "We are building a canoe in which everyone is welcome [to stop the pipeline and protect the environment]." George then joined the chiefs of more than one hundred First Nations in signing the Save the Fraser Declaration, which called for a ban on pipelines through First Nations territories and on tankers travelling the ocean migration routes of Fraser River salmon.

Later that summer, a flotilla of about a dozen First Nations ocean-going canoes paddled under the Lions Gate and Second Narrows Bridges to the oil terminal and then to Cates Park in opposition to the proposed pipeline and tanker traffic expansion. While paddlers wearing T-shirts reading "Protect the Salish Sea: Many People One Canoe" watched, chiefs from two First Nations signed a Declaration of Opposition to the proposal. The 2014 Tribal Journeys to Bella Bella is being presented as an opportunity "to pull together with other coastal indigenous people to save the Great Bear Rainforest."[11]

It is perhaps appropriate that canoes are being used to protest new oil transportation plans, as they are one of the few forms of transportation today that don't require petroleum as their energy source. Indeed, the various traditional canoes represent very sustainable forms of transportation: the materials used to make them were locally replenished, the human or wind energy to power them was renewable, and they could be naturally "recycled" at the end of their useful life.

Looking more broadly, the canoe used by Aboriginal people in BC prior to contact with Europeans was at the heart of a sustainable economy. The resources people depended upon were primarily renewable and treated with respect to ensure their ongoing ability to support the population. By contrast, the Europeans introduced an economy that depended upon non-sustainable levels of resource use, often to the point of exhaustion, followed by repeating the process in a new area, usually farther west. In BC this can be seen in the harvesting of sea otters to virtual extinction; the felling of old-growth trees, often by clear-cutting; and the extraction of minerals, such as during short-lived gold rushes. In many cases, the rapid harvesting of the resources for overseas markets was to support forms of conspicuous consumption rather than meeting basic human needs.

These opposite approaches to natural-resource use have not gone unnoticed. During Reconciliation Canada's canoe gathering, Frank Brown, who had such a big role in the resurgence of the ocean-going dugout canoes, said:

> At this time in human history, when people are so very, very concerned about the sustainability and resiliency of this planet, it is the values of our people that will lead humanity forward if you will but listen to us, the indigenous people, who have something to share. Be kind to the earth, be kind to the sea.

David Suzuki, paddling in another canoe that day, later responded from the water:

> The First Nations people have hung on to something that we desperately need. We have got a bad model of what progress and development is all about and we are undermining the very life-support systems of the planet in the name of development and growth and the First Nations people have something different . . . They are telling us there are things more important than money. We have an opportunity to reach reconciliation and to learn from these people who have held on to their values and their culture and who know that we are created out of Mother Earth.

Although the canoe has been used to symbolize a variety of things in Canada, the recurring current symbolism in British

Columbia is that of unity—unity among people and unity with nature. This can be seen in both the artistic portrayals of the canoe and the way the craft is being used in the province and beyond.

Perhaps the ultimate form of canoe symbolism, however, is that for spiritual purposes. Aboriginal people have long viewed the canoe as a spiritual vessel. Ceremonies prior to the launch of a canoe or a canoeing event are common in First Nations cultures throughout the region. Some even believe that a spiritual canoe transports the dead to another world. It is no wonder that BC First Nations people strongly resist calling the canoe a "boat" since it represents so much more for them.[12]

Although they come from many religious backgrounds, local dragon boat and outrigger canoe racers, as we have seen, have practices reflecting the spiritual heritages of their craft. Speaking about the traditional birchbark-style canoe, Bill Mason said, "It is as if God made the canoe and then set about creating a country in which it could flourish. That country was Canada."[13] The more common Caucasian perspective is not so much that the canoe is a spiritual vessel as that it is one that can take people on a spiritual journey. Former prime minister Pierre Elliott Trudeau, an avid canoeist, wrote, "Paddling a canoe is a source of enrichment and inner renewal. It carries a man into the truest part of himself."[14] In his foreword to a book by Bill Mason, Trudeau wrote, "May every dip of your paddle lead you toward a rediscovery of yourself, of your canoeing companions, of the wonders of nature, and of the unmatched physical and spiritual rapture made possible by the humble canoe."[15]

chapter seven

CONCLUDING STROKES

WHEN we moved to British Columbia from Ontario, I knew about the canoes that came to this province from the East—the birchbark-style craft, whose basic design has endured despite variations in length and an evolution of building materials. But I now know about the dragon boats and outrigger canoes that came from across the Pacific ocean; the kayak, umiak, and Kootenay canoes that originated in the North; and the Salish racing canoes that were developed locally and farther south, making BC a veritable canoe crossroads. And in another dimension, I learned about the novel kayak that was built here and named after the highest point in the province, known historically as "the paddler's mountain."

I have seen all these current types of canoes at various times at my local oceanfront park, and sometimes—like at the canoe gathering in False Creek during Vancouver's Reconciliation Week— they all converge at the same time and place, making a powerful impact. The crossing of these different types of canoes, with their varied backgrounds and current roles, is interesting enough, but I find the underlying themes found throughout the BC canoe family particularly intriguing.

The first such theme is the role canoes have played in the province's creation. Skin canoes, specifically kayaks and umiaks, likely enabled the first people to reach the Americas, via the west coast, and begin human civilization on these continents. Dugout canoes then facilitated the development of a thriving First Nations culture and supported a sustainable economy in this province. Later, birchbark canoes brought people to the province from the East, enabling exploration, fur trading, and other forms of enterprise, which helped establish the northern and southern boundaries of the province.

Canoes are the result of creative ingenuity in using local materials to meet people's needs in their varying environments. Historically, the ocean-going dugout canoes were both beautiful and practical vessels that could face the rigours of the open ocean. Later, David Thompson fashioned cedar-plank river canoes here when he couldn't find birchbark and may well have introduced this design back in Ontario, where it blossomed. And the Salish people developed long, sleek racing canoes for their own needs and to circumvent laws preventing their gathering for non-sporting purposes.

More recently, innovative canoes using modern materials have been created in British Columbia. The early BC designers and builders of seagoing kayaks were leaders in the resurgence of this historic craft. Vincent Lo's Six-Sixteen dragon boats were the first fibreglass ones in the world more than forty feet long. Western Canoeing and Kayaking's Sea-1 was a novel combination of canoe and kayak that served one marathon paddler well as he faced the varying conditions in a cross-Canada paddle. And Chris Cooper's

Spirit Dancer, which amalgamated features from birchbark, dugout, and kayak canoes, proved to be up to the task of handling the open Atlantic and Pacific Oceans.

BC designers and builders have also produced some of the smallest and largest modern canoes in the world. Doug Simpson's Feathercraft makes open-ocean-worthy kayaks that can fit in a backpack while George Dyson built the world's largest kayak to take him to Alaska. James van Nostrand designed the sixty-five-foot fibreglass ocean-going canoe that is billed as the largest canoe in North America. And Western Canoeing and Kayaking, in addition to manufacturing that craft, is the largest "big canoe" builder in the world with its line of voyageur and ocean-going canoes of varying sizes.

The canoes created in BC have often travelled well beyond the province, radiating outwards in all directions. Bill Reid's *Spirit of Haida Gwaii* sculpture now resides in the capitals of both Canada and the US, in addition to the Vancouver International Airport. His original dugout canoe, *Lootaas*, has been to Paris, while Chris Cooper's *Spirit Dancer* has travelled north to Alaska and from London around much of the UK. West Vancouver's dugout canoe *Orenda* has paddled and sailed all the way to Hawaii, following in the footsteps of the dugout canoe–hulled *Tilikum* that travelled west from Victoria to London. And one of Western's modern seventeen-foot canoes completed one of the longest canoe trips ever made—over twenty thousand kilometres from Calgary to Belém, Brazil.

A second theme that runs through BC canoes is development—of individuals and communities. Canoe racers have reported developing personal skills and the ability to work in groups. Certainly there are lots of opportunities for canoe racing in BC, with event organizers claiming the largest voyageur canoe race in the world, the largest weekly paddlesport race in

North America, and one of the largest dragon boat festivals on this continent. Some of our racers have been the best in the world, including Hugh Fisher in sprint kayaking, Pemberton teenagers in dragon boating, and False Creek Racing Canoe Club members in outrigger canoeing.

These benefits have not been limited to racers, as similar skill development has been reported by those involved in longer outings such as the annual Tribal Journeys trips in big canoes and *Spirit Dancer's* travels along different coasts. Indeed, the benefits have been felt even beyond the participants in these activities and have extended to whole communities. The Tribal Journeys trips galvanize not only the paddlers themselves, but also the hosts at the visited communities. These trips have encouraged a renewed awareness of and pride in First Nations culture and of being part of a canoe nation. UBC's Day of the Longboat races raise the spirit and sense of identity beyond those in the canoes to the broader university community. And when Steven Point carved a canoe when he was BC's Lieutenant-Governor, it conveyed the need to work together in a wider community.

A third theme that weaves through canoes in BC is the role they have played in healing. For individuals, a wonderful example is the breast cancer dragon boat teams that started here and have spread around the world, even inspiring similar groups to raise awareness of other medical conditions. These teams not only provide exercise for their members, but also serve as floating support groups and a means of educating the broader public on relevant prevention strategies. For physically healthy individuals, longer canoe trips can heal the spirit, allowing paddlers to return with a greater sense of clarity and purpose.

Canoes have also facilitated healing between groups of people who have historically strained or oppressive relationships. Just as the voyageur canoes that first travelled here from across the country comprised people of different cultures speaking different languages, dragon boats were introduced to Canada via British Columbia as a means of improving relations between newly arrived Asians and those from other backgrounds. Similarly, the canoe gathering prior to the hearings of the Truth and Reconciliation Commission in Vancouver united representatives from First Nations, churches, and police agencies—symbolizing a willingness to grapple with the devastation caused by the residential school experience together.

More broadly, canoes have helped heal our relationship with nature. Sometimes this has involved raising awareness—whether through student canoe trips on the Fraser River or along the Pacific coast, or through prominent works of art that symbolically place the human and the animal world in one canoe. And sometimes it has involved political protest such as using canoe flotillas to demonstrate opposition to planned pipeline and oil tanker routes.

The artwork on the cover of this book—*Skookum Kalitan*, a lithograph by Ed Hill—captures these three themes well. Hill is a retired member of the RCMP who organized and paddled in VisionQuest, the 1997 journey led by the RCMP from Hazelton to Victoria described in Chapter 2. *Skookum Kalitan* was the RCMP canoe on that journey and one that I had a chance to paddle thirteen years later.

The three canoes on that journey were the first Northern Dancers produced by BC's Western Canoeing and Kayaking. These canoes were inspired by the resurgence of the ocean-going dugout canoes in BC and by the fibreglass outrigger canoes in Hawaii. Western took the design of the dugouts and the material of the outriggers to create something totally new—a fibreglass ocean-going canoe. These canoes, which were lighter and easier to maintain than their cedar counterparts, were initially greeted with considerable skepticism. They soon gained acceptance, however, and have now spread throughout BC and beyond, prompting Western to make different-sized versions of these craft.

The people paddling on the VisionQuest journey had intense experiences and considerable personal development, as evident in Ed Hill's comments on pages 141–43. This trip inspired the annual Pulling Together journeys, with *Skookum Kalitan* as a regular participant, in which at-risk First Nations teens paddled alongside adults, who were often from police or other government agencies. The T-shirts with the slogan "Canoeing Saved My Life . . . Ask Me How" worn by some of the youth on the trips symbolized the personal development they experienced as they worked alongside a new group of adults and experienced their own culture in a new and inspiring way.

The story behind Hill's lithograph also reflects the theme of healing. The VisionQuest journey was organized by two individuals who had struggled with substance abuse, and it was designed to bring attention to this problem in society and to raise funds to support a recovery centre in BC. This was the start of a movement that led to the establishment of a string of recovery houses operated by the VisionQuest Recovery Society throughout the province. The journey was also an opportunity for the RCMP to apologize to First Nations communities for enforcing earlier government policies affecting these communities and to begin to heal the relationships with those communities. It was only fitting, then, that when the RCMP decided to buy a new canoe and *Skookum Kalitan* was to be sold to an American buyer, a BC community raised the funds to keep it in the province.

In concluding this look at the role of the canoe in BC, I hope it has become apparent that canoes have played—and continue to play—an important role in shaping this province. While the canoe is often associated with Canada as a whole, and perhaps particularly with Ontario, it is evident that canoes, broadly defined, have had a big impact on BC and that there is a strong canoe culture here today.

I'm still somewhat mystified about why, as discussed in the Introduction, Canadians and particularly British Columbians do not readily identify the canoe as an important symbol of Canada. After all, a CBC panel named the canoe a Wonder of Canada and the Canadian Government chose a modern BC canoe sculpture for its main artwork at its Washington embassy. Perhaps the canoe is so pervasive in our past and present that we are not fully conscious of its significance. But in my observation of and participation in canoe events, I have seen the craft's ability to bring people together—to break down cultural boundaries, open up the lines of communication, encourage teamwork, and foster a greater connection with nature. Whether on river, lake, or sea; whether made of plant, animal, or man-made materials; and whether used for pleasure, racing, or symbolic purposes, the canoe has been instrumental in creating, developing, and healing in this province. And it will continue to be a powerful presence for many years to come.

APPENDIX
SKOOKUM KALITAN

THE summer of 1997 will, for me, be a time that is forever etched in the warmest corner of my mind. It was a summer of dreams and aspirations, a summer of goals, and a time of personal tests and achievements. Perhaps most of all, though, it was a summer of intense emotions.

That was the summer that the RCMP and my friend Roy Henry Vickers embarked on a joint venture. Together, along with members of the public, we paddled three canoes three hundred kilometres down the Skeena River from Hazelton to Prince Rupert. From Prince Rupert, we pulled those three craft all the way to Victoria. The one-month journey consisted of sixteen hundred kilometres of indelible experience. It was all being done under the auspices of VisionQuest, a non-profit society, formed by Vickers and the RCMP. Its purpose was to bring the issues of addiction in our society to the fore. Its ultimate goal was to accrue sufficient funds to build a recovery centre for all addictions, for all people, here on the west coast of Canada.

Our journey in those canoes would take us through times of tears and laughter. We would weather personal storms of frustration and anger. We would languish in favouring winds and tides, and we would toil against raging river waters and twenty-foot-high waves. Each evening we would step wide-eyed from the canoe into the distant past as we entered native villages greeted by age-old ceremony and traditional feasts that have been enjoyed for centuries on this coast. Lifelong friendships developed, and equally intense relationships were forged with those who we may never see again in this life. Like some flash of a camera, those moments will be seared in my mind's eye to linger always.

My canoe, the one that I sat and worked in for the entire journey, was *Skookum Kalitan*. It was owned by the RCMP. No matter what my emotions, as I waded into the waters to enter the canoe each morning, it washed those emotions away and brought me back to a constant. The canoe is such a special place, particularly when it takes you so far and experiences so much with you. The constant I always returned to was one of a calm reassurance, a sense of being in the proper place at the proper time. *Skookum Kalitan* had a sense of "home" to it. It had a personality. We had long been told by the Native people that a canoe represents community, and that is truly how it felt. No matter what the task at hand, no matter what issues or problems we were leaving on the shore or were awaiting us at the next beach, *Skookum Kalitan* provided the warm, comfortable feeling of community. So real and intense was the feeling in that canoe, I can only look with eager anticipation to the next time I will pull it to some distant shore. To this day I cannot watch videos of that canoe, see photographs of the summer of 1997, or talk of the events of that month, without stirring intense emotions within me.

Throughout the journey of the summer of '97, I kept a journal about the experience. In it, I recalled my last day of the trip when everyone else had left save a few of us to clean up. For the first time in five months of training, preparation, and travel, the canoe was finished its job. It had been lifted from the waters of Victoria Harbour and was awaiting its trailer ride back to Vancouver. I awoke early that morning and stepped from my tent to see the canoe on the grass of our campsite. These words are found in my journal, dated Day 37, August 4, 1997:

It lay there listing to one side. I could see that there was virtually nothing inside it. There were no water bottles awaiting today's pull. No paddles rested over the seats. No life vests sat waiting for the day. It was empty and lifeless. That friend that had been so alive and vital for five months now was lifeless. It was an inanimate "thing," not a place of peace and happiness. I turned my head to an empty parking lot and then looked back at the canoe. IT HIT! IT HIT HARD!

The image I have painted is in memory and recognition of that friend. It is a recognition of a historic time, but most of all, it is truly my emotions on paper. I will forever remember the summer of 1997, the summer of dreams, and I will never forget my friend *Skookum Kalitan*.

—ED HILL, artist

ACKNOWLEDGEMENTS

THIS, my first book, has been a lifetime in the making. I want to thank my parents, Gordon and Nancy Osler, who first introduced me to the canoe, and to all the people I have since paddled with who provided me with such rich memories involving the canoe.

The idea of writing a book about canoes started to form with presentations I gave on the subject beginning about six years ago, and I want to thank all those who showed interest in the talks and encouraged me to continue to tell the story of the canoe in British Columbia. I particularly want to thank Daniel Francis and Howard White, who thought there was potential for a book on the subject and suggested ways to structure it, and to Bobbi Linkemer for the guidance provided in her *How to Write a Nonfiction Book: From Concept to Completion in 6 Months.*

The best part of writing the book was the researching phase, where I had the opportunity to talk to so many interesting people about canoes. Many are identified in the book, but special thanks for going above and beyond answering my questions go to Mike Billy, Chris Cooper, Ed Hill, and Karyn Lippincott. Similarly, collecting beautiful images of the canoe was a wonderful phase, and I am very grateful to all those who offered them, particularly professional photographers Carter Brundage, Pam Mullins, Lester Picker and Dave Speers, who did so without remuneration, as did professional artist Ed Hill, who contributed the striking image on the cover.

I was fortunate to have support from the Nonfiction Authors Association and the North Shore Writers Association, and from professional editors Iva Cheung, Talia Leduc, and Patricia Wolfe during the initial writing phase. I also appreciated the feedback and encouragement from two friends, Ken Gill and Franz Scherubl, who faithfully read every chapter as it came off the computer. Jesse Finkelstein, Lucy Kenward, Nadine Pedersen, and Sylvia Taylor also provided invaluable advice and assistance in the search for a publisher.

That search led to Heritage House Publishing in Victoria, which showed strong interest in my proposal and have supported me through to completion. Special thanks go to editor Lara Kordic, who not only edited the book but also served as project manager and as my teacher about the publishing process; publisher Rodger Touchie, for his willingness to take a risk on a new author; and designer Jacqui Thomas, who made the book look beautiful.

And finally I want to thank my immediate family for their support of this venture: my son, Matthew, with whom I did my early canoe trips in BC and who later was a great sounding board and advisor about the book, my daughter, Lynn, who used her communications degree to help me communicate more broadly about this book, and my wife, Betty Ann, whose love and support allowed me to pursue my dream of telling the story of the canoe in British Columbia.

ENDNOTES

INTRODUCTION

1. Peter Mansbridge, Seven Wonders of Canada show, CBC TV, July 1, 2007.
2. Tobin Dalrymple, "Unifying a nation under a cherished symbol: The Maple Leaf has come to define Canada, poll reveals," *Vancouver Sun*, June 30, 2008. A5.
3. Amy Husser, "We may grumble—but we identify with that Maple Leaf," *Vancouver Sun*, June 27, 2008. A9.
4. From www.canoeicf.com, History section, July 3, 2007.
5. Kenneth G. Roberts and Philip Shackleton, *The Canoe: A History of the Craft from Panama to the Arctic* (Toronto: Macmillan of Canada, 1983), 2.

CHAPTER 1: THE BIRCHBARK CANOE

1. Display at Canadian Canoe Museum.
2. John Jennings, *Bark Canoes: The Art and Obsession of Tappan Adney* (Richmond Hill, ON: Firefly Books, 2004), 139.
3. Display at Canadian Canoe museum.
4. Jennings, *Bark Canoes*, 139.
5. John Murray Gibbon, *The Romance of the Canadian Canoe* (Toronto: Ryerson Press, 1969), 67–68.
6. Bruce Hutchison, *The Fraser* (Vancouver: Clarke, Irwin & Company Limited, 1950), 34.
7. Gibbon, *Romance*, 89.
8. Roberts and Shackleton, *The Canoe*, 235.
9. Ibid., 235–36.
10. James Raffan, *Bark, Skin and Cedar: Exploring the Canoe in Canadian Experience* (Toronto: Harper Collins, 1999), 73.

11. From clippercanoes.com/boat_specs.php?model_id=105

12. *Globe and Mail*, "Canoe president 'like Mr. Ambassador for Canada,'" June 30, 2011.

CHAPTER 2: THE DUGOUT CANOE

1. Martine Reid, *Bill Reid and the Haida Canoe* (Madeira Park, BC: Harbour Publishing, 2011), 73.

2. Heather Ramsay and Kwiaahwah Jones, comps. and eds., *Gina 'Waadluxan Tluu: The Everything Canoe* (Skidegate, BC: Haida Gwaii Museum Press, 2010), 31.

3. Roberts and Shackleton, *The Canoe*, 97.

4. Hilary Stewart, *Cedar: Tree of Life to the Northwest Coast Indians* (Vancouver: Douglas & McIntyre, 1984), 48.

5. Roberts and Shackleton, *The Canoe*, 97.

6. Stewart, *Cedar*, 48.

7. Roberts and Shackleton, *The Canoe*, 99.

8. William Henry Collison, *In the Wake of the War Canoe*. Edited and Annotated by Charles Lillard. (Victoria: Sono Nis Press, 1981), 54.

9. Ibid., 95

10. Raffan, *Bark, Skin and Cedar: Exploring the Canoe in Canadian Experience* (Toronto: Harper Collins, 1999), 214.

11. Bill Reid from an exhibit at the Bill Reid Northwest Coast Art Gallery.

12. Reid, *Bill Reid*, 105.

13. Ibid., 109.

14. Ibid., 94.

15. David Neel, *The Great Canoes: Reviving a Northwest Coast Tradition* (Vancouver: Douglas & McIntyre, 1995), 127.

16. *Qatuwas 2014: Tribal Journeys to Bella Bella*.

17. Neel, *The Great Canoes*, 127–28.

18. Ibid., 51.

19. Ibid., 125.

20. Ibid., 59.

21. Ibid., 98.

22. Ibid., 127.

23. "Science added to native trek," *Vancouver Sun*, July 15, 2008.

24. Ursula Vaira, *And See What Happens: the journey poems*. (Halfmoon Bay, BC: Caitlin Press, 2011), 33.

25. Vaira, *And See What Happens*, 26.

26. Jody Paterson, "Mounties found tears and reconciliation," *Times Colonist*, August 2, 1997.

27. Justine Hunter, "In the same boat: canoe journey pulls together officers and aboriginal youth," *Globe and Mail*, July 9, 2011, S4.

28. Ibid., S4.

CHAPTER 3: THE SKIN CANOE

1. John Jennings, *The Canoe: A Living Tradition* (Toronto: Firefly Books, 2002), 136.

2. Ibid., 136–37.

3. Ibid., 131–32.

4. Edwin Tappan Adney and Howard Chapelle, *Bark Canoes and Skin Boats of North America* (Washington: Smithsonian Institution, 1964), 192.

5. Roberts and Shackleton, *The Canoe*, 136.

6. Ibid., 136.

7. Ibid., 137.

8. Ibid., 138.

9. George Dyson, *Baidarka: The Kayak* (Seattle, WA: Alaska Northwest Books, 1997), xiii.

10. Ibid., 127.

11. Ibid., 89.

12. Ibid., 90.

13. Ibid., 166.

14. Kenneth Brower, *The Starship and the Canoe* (New York: Holt, Rinehart and Winston, 1978), 186.

15. Ibid., 196.

16. Dyson, *Baidarka*, 106.

17. Ibid., 107.

18. Ibid., x.

19. Ibid., 216.

20. Ibid., 143.

21. Brower, *The Starship and the Canoe*, 264.

22. Ibid., 146.

23. Interview with the author, November 24, 2013.

24. British Columbia Achievement Foundation, "BC recognizes top achievers," British Columbia Achievement Foundation, bcachievement.com.

25. From feathercraft.com/raves-reviews.

26. Tim Shuff, "The Early Years," *Adventure Kayak Magazine* (Summer 2004).

27. Ibid.

28. From clippercanoes.com/cross_canada.php and interview with the author on November 25, 2013.

29. From www.canoekayak.com posted on September 1, 2010.

CHAPTER 4: THE FIRST CANOES

1. Interviewed in Clare Duncan and Peter Oxley, *The Incredible Human Journey: The Americas* (London: BBC Television, 2009).

2. Interview with the author on November 9, 2012.

3. Edward J. Vajda, "The Dene-Yeniseian Connection" in *Anthropological Papers of the University of Alaska*, New Series, Vol.: 1–2, 2010, 100–18.

4. *Vancouver Sun*, April 3, 2008.

5. N. Misarti, B.P. Finney, J.W. Jordan, H.D. Maschner, J.A. Addison, M.D. Shapley, A. Krumhardt and J.E. Beget. "Early retreat of the Alaska Peninsula Glacier Complex and the implications for coastal migrations of First Americans." *Quarterly Science Reviews* 48, 2012, 1–6.

6. Duncan and Oxley, *The Incredible Journey*.

7. *UVic knowlEDGE* 3 2003.

8. Ted Goebel, Michael R. Waters and Dennis H. O'Rourke, "The Late Pleistocene Dispersal of Modern Humans in the Americas," *Science* 319, no. 5869, 2008, 1497–1502.

9. John Jennings, Bruce W. Hodgins and Doreen Small, eds., *The Canoe in Canadian Culture*. (Winnipeg: Natural Heritage/Natural History Inc., 1999), 44.

10. Fred Bruemmer, "Last of the Umiaks," *Natural History Magazine*, October, 1992.

11. Ibid.

12. Ibid.

13. Ibid.

14. Ibid.

15. Roberts and Shackleton, *The Canoe*, 145.

16. Jennings, *The Canoe*, 153.

17. Jennings, Hodgins and Small, *The Canoe in Canadian Culture*, 44.

18. Bruemmer, "Last of the Umiaks."

19. Roberts and Shackleton, *The Canoe*, 105.

20. *Seattle Times*, October 27, 1998.

21. Jon M. Erlandson et al. "The Kelp Highway Hypothesis: Marine Ecology, the Coastal Migration Theory, and the Peopling of the Americas," *The Journal of Island and Coastal Archaeology* 2(2), 2007, 161–74.

22. Duncan and Oxley, *The Incredible Journey*.

23. Wynne Parry, "Oregon cave discovery suggests lost ancient American culture" in *The Christian Science Monitor*, July 12, 2012.

24. Daryl W. Fedje and Rolf W. Mathewes, eds. *Haida Gwaii: Human History and Environment from the Time of Loon to the Time of the Iron Man* (Vancouver: UBC Press, 2005), xvii.

CHAPTER 5: RACING CANOES

1. CanoeKayakBC, *2009–2010 Annual Report*, 6.

2. There is another type of "war canoe," which holds fifteen people and is paddled while kneeling on one knee. This thirty foot canoe was introduced in the East in the late 1800s and is still popular at some summer camps and canoeing clubs there. It is not very common in BC now, but interest in this team sport is growing among adults here.

3. Personal interview with Stanley ("Spin") Thomas, March 21, 2013.

4. Virtual Museum of Canada, Coast Salish Canoe Racing in *Living Traditions: Museums Honour the North American Indigenous Games*. museevirtuel-virtualmuseum.ca/sgc-cms/expositions-exhibitions/traditions/English/salish_canoe_08. html. Accessed March 28, 2013.

5. Personal interview with Mike Billy, April 19, 2013

6. Ibid.

7. Tsleil-Waututh Nation, *The Richard M. George Memorial Canoe Race*, July 9–10, 2011, 2.

8. Citizenship and Immigration Canada, cic.gc.ca/english/multiculturalism/asian/20 years.asp. Accessed March 8, 2013.

9. Heather Kent, "Mr. Dragon Boat," *Canadian Medical Association Journal*, 167 (9), 2002: 1048.

10. Phone interview with Tachona Jones on October 10, 2013.

CHAPTER 6: SYMBOLIC CANOES

1. Jennings, *The Canoe in Canadian Culture*, 1.

2. Daniel Francis, *National Dreams: Myth, Memory, and Canadian History*, (Vancouver: Arsenal Pulp Press, 1997), 151.

3. Shannon Moneo, "How to really carve a name for yourself," *Globe and Mail*, Sept. 16, 2009: S2.

4. Dirk Meissner, "Point leaves office on high note," *Globe and Mail*, Nov. 1, 2012.

5. The cargo ship is based on the four that arrived in the late 1990s from China's Fujian Province carrying six hundred migrants seeking refuge status.

6.   The *Komagata Maru* was a steamship that attempted in 1914 to unload 376 British subjects, passengers from Punjab, India, in Vancouver. Only 24 were admitted to Canada and the ship was forced to return to India with the remaining passengers due to laws aimed at excluding immigrants from that country.

7.   Brent Richter, "City OKs res school monument," *North Shore News*, Sept. 11, 2013: 1.

8.   Dawn Green, "The call of the wild," *Pique Newsmagazine*, August 23, 2012: 45.

9.   From northerndevelopment.bc.ca/explore-our-region/success-stories/metlakatla-embarks-on-a-canoe-quest on October 1, 2013.

10.   From worldriversday.com on October 2, 2013.

11.   *Qatuwas 2014: Tribal Journeys to Bella Bella.*

12.   See, for example, Neel, *The Great Canoes*, 1.

13.   Bill Mason from an exhibit at the Canadian Canoe Museum, Peterborough, Ontario.

14.   Pierre Trudeau in a note to Dr. Joe MacInnis.

15.   Pierre Trudeau in Bill Mason, *Path of the Paddle: An Illustrated Guide to the Art of Canoeing* (Toronto: Van Nostrand Reinhold Ltd., 1980), v.

BIBLIOGRAPHY

Alberni District Historical Society. *Place Names of the Alberni Valley*. Port Alberni, BC, 1988.

Adney, Edwin Tappan and Chapelle, Howard I. *Bark Canoes and Skin Boats of North America*. Washington: Smithsonian Institution, 1964.

Baidarka. Camden, Maine: Ragged Mountain Press, 1995.

Barker, Pat. *Dragon Boats: A Celebration*. Vancouver: Raincoast Books, 1996.

Benidickson, Jamie. *Idleness, Water, and a Canoe: Reflections on Paddling for Pleasure*. Toronto: University of Toronto Press, 1997.

Blandford, Percy W. *Canoeing*. London: W. & G. Foyle Ltd., 1959.

———. *Tackle Canoeing*, London: Stanley Paul & Co. Ltd., 1961.

Brinck, Wolfgand. *The Aleutian Kayak: Origins, Construction, and Use of the Traditional Seagoing Baidarka*. Camden, Maine: Ragged Mountain Press, 1995.

Bringhurst, Robert (text) and Ulli Steltzer (photographs). *The Black Canoe: Bill Reid and the Spirit of Haida Gwaii*. Vancouver: Douglas & McIntyre Ltd., 1991.

Brower, Kenneth, *The Starship and the Canoe*, New York: Holt, Rinehart and Winston, 1978.

Brown, Frank and Y. Kathy Brown. *Staying the Course, Staying Alive—Coastal First Nations Fundamental Truths: Biodiversity, Stewardship and Sustainability*. Victoria: Biodiversity BC, 2009.

Cody, Robin. *Voyage of a Summer Sun: Canoeing the Columbia River*. Seattle: Sasquatch Books, 1996.

Collison, William Henry. *In the Wake of the War Canoe*. Edited and Annotated by Charles Lillard. Victoria: Sono Nis Press, 1981.

Dyson, George B. *Baidarka: The Kayak*. Seattle, WA: Alaska Northwest Books, 1997.

Fedje, Daryl W. and Rolf W. Mathewes, eds. *Haida Gwaii: Human History and Environment from the Time of Loon to the Time of the Iron Man*. Vancouver: University of British Columbia Press, 2005.

Fischer, David Hackett. *Champlain's Dream: The Visionary Adventurer who made a New World in Canada*. Toronto: Alfred A. Knopf Canada, 2008.

Francis, Daniel. *National Dreams: Myth, Memory, and Canadian History*. Vancouver: Arsenal Pulp Press, 1997.

Gibbon, John Murray, *The Romance of the Canadian Canoe*. Toronto: Ryerson Press, 1951.

Holling, Holling Clancy. *Paddle-to-the Sea*. Boston: Houghton Mifflin, 1969.

Hume, Stephen. *Simon Fraser: In Search of Modern British Columbia*. Madeira Park, BC: Harbour Publishing, 2008.

Hutchinson, Bruce. *The Fraser*. Vancouver: Clarke, Irwin & Company Limited, 1950.

Jennings, John. *Bark Canoes: The Art and Obsession of Tappan Adney*. Richmond Hill, ON: Firefly Books, 2004.

———. *The Canoe: A Living Tradition*. Toronto: Firefly Books, 2002.

Jennings, John, Bruce W. Hodgins, and Doreen Small, eds. *The Canoe in Canadian Culture*. Winnipeg: Natural Heritage/Natural History Inc., 1999.

Lincoln, Leslie, *Coast Salish Canoes*. Seattle: The Center for Wooden Boats, 1999.

Mason, Bill. *Path of the Paddle: An Illustrated Guide to the Art of Canoeing*. Toronto: Van Nostrand and Reinhold, 1980.

McFarlane, Peter and Wayne Haimila. *Ancient Land, Ancient Sky: Following Canada's Canoe Routes*. Toronto: Alfred A. Knopf Canada, 1999.

Moores, Ted. *KayakCraft: Fine Woodstrip Kayak Construction*. Brooklin, Maine: WoodenBoat Publications, 1999.

Morse, Eric W. *Fur Trade Canoe Routes of Canada/Then and Now*. Ottawa: National and Historic Parks Branch, 1971.

Neel, David, *The Great Canoes: Reviving a Northwest Coast Tradition*. Vancouver: Douglas & McIntyre, 1995.

Poole, Michael. *Ragged Islands: A Journey by Canoe Through the Inside Passage*. Vancouver: Douglas & McIntyre, 1991.

Raffan, James. *Bark, Skin and Cedar: Exploring the Canoe in Canadian Experience*. Toronto: Harper Collins, 1999.

Raffan, James and Bert Horwood, eds. *Canexus: The Canoe in Canadian Culture*. Toronto: Betelgeuse Books, 1988.

Ramsay, Heather and Kwiaahwah Jones, comps. and eds. *Gina 'Waadluxan Tluu: The Everything Canoe*. Skidegate, BC: Haida Gwaii Museum Press, 2010.

Reid, Martine J., ed. *Bill Reid and the Haida Canoe*. Madeira Park, BC: Harbour Publishing, 2011.

Roberts, Kenneth G. and Philip Shackleton. *The Canoe: A History of the Craft from Panama to the Arctic*. Toronto: Macmillan of Canada, 1983.

Saul, John Ralston. *A Fair Country: Telling Truths about Canada*. Toronto: Viking Canada, 2008.

Solway, Kenneth, *The Story of the Chestnut Canoe: 150 Years of Canadian Canoe Building*. Halifax: Nimbus Publishing, 1997.

Starkell, Don and Charles Wilkens, ed., *Paddle to the Amazon: The Ultimate 12,000-mile Canoe Adventure*. Toronto: McClelland and Stewart, 1987.

Stewart, Hilary. *Cedar: Tree of Life to the Northwest Coast Indians*. Vancouver: Douglas & McIntyre, 1984.

Twigger, Robert. *Voyageur: Across the Rocky Mountains in a Birchbark Canoe*. London: Weidenfeld & Nicolson, 2006.

Vaira, Ursula. *And See What Happens: the journey poems*. Halfmoon Bay, BC: Caitlin Press, 2011.

Vajda, Edward J. "The Dene-Yeniseian Connection" in *Anthropological Papers of the University of Alaska*, New Series, Vol. 5:1-2. 2010, 100–18.

INDEX

THE DREAM
ELITA KUSTOM CONFIG

ERIC STARTUP

PARKIES BUILD **ABOUT THE AUTHOR**

BRADZ LITE BUILD V1
THE WIZARD   XENON

SANFORD OSLER was introduced to canoes as a youngster at summer camp, an event that sparked a lifelong interest in the role of the canoe in our history and modern-day lives. This fascination has led him to collect research and information about the subject over many years, and he has given talks about the canoe to audiences across BC. Osler has owned a red sixteen-foot wooden canoe for over forty years and has taken it on trips throughout Canada, including the Broken Islands, Bowron Lakes, and Gulf Islands. He holds an MA from the University of British Columbia and is currently chair of the North Vancouver Museum and Archives Commission and a trustee of the North Vancouver District Public Library. For more information, visit sanfordosler.ca.

RAYS BUILD 0.0.6
GREEN FROG
THR ARDS BUILD